YOU MAY ALL PROPHESY

STEVE THOMPSON

MorningStar Publications
A DIVISION OF MORNINGSTAR FELLOWSHIP CHURCH
375 Star Light Drive, Fort Mill, SC 29715
www.MorningStarMinistries.org

You May All Prophesy
Copyright © 2000 by Steve Thompson
2nd Printing Mass Market edition, 2007

Distributed by MorningStar Publications, Inc.,
a division of MorningStar Fellowship Church
375 Star Light Drive, Fort Mill, SC 29715
www.MorningStarMinistries.org

International Standard Book Number: 1-59933-089-x, 978-1-59933-089-1

Cover Design: Kevin Lepp
Book Layout: Sharon Whitby
For information call 1-800-542-0278.

Unless otherwise indicated, all Scripture quotations are taken from the New American Standard Bible, copyright © 1960, 1962, 1963, 1968, 1971, 1973, 1974, 1977 by The Lockman Foundation. Italics in Scripture are for emphasis only.

This book is dedicated to
Rick Joyner and Bob Jones,
who are spiritual fathers to many.
Your friendship and mentoring
have encouraged and refined me.
Your example of faith, humility,
and devotion to the Lord
has convicted and inspired me.
I owe you a debt I could never repay.

TABLE OF CONTENTS

Chapter One
THE BASICS OF PROPHECY

While praying for a husband and wife, Matt received a prophetic word for them and began telling them things he could not have known naturally. He told the woman that she had three children, but that her oldest, a son, had gone away. He then said to her, "Your oldest has gone away, but the Lord wants you to know that his heart is in the hand of the Lord." The lady began weeping and worshiping God. Her husband looked stunned and began to weep also. Their friends who surrounded them began rejoicing.

They did have three children, and the oldest was indeed a son. However, the previous year he had drowned while swimming off the Mediterranean coast. He had drifted from the Lord in the years prior to his death and had been estranged from his parents as well. They had been tormented since his death, not knowing the state of his heart toward the Lord, due to their limited contact with him. Their hearts were comforted and healed through this prophetic word.

What value can be placed on a prophetic word like this? A mother and father were delivered from torment concerning their child and given new confidence in God's love for them. Obviously, there is no price tag that can be placed on any single prophetic word like this. It is literally priceless.

When I first met Matt, he was tentative to give even the simplest prophetic words, much less something of this magnitude. However, with training, encouragement, and opportunities to "try his wings," he has become an anointed prophetic minister. He is only one of several thousand who have been trained through our congregation and similar prophetic training seminars we have sponsored.

BUT WHAT ABOUT...?

Questions about prophecy and the prophetic ministry abound. Is the prophetic ministry valid for today? Who can prophesy? How does God speak? How do you know when God is speaking to you? What about prophecies that do not come to pass? If a word is not 100 percent accurate, is the person who gave the word a false prophet? Is it permissible to ask God for dreams, visions, and words?

This book will address these questions and others, as well as examine how God speaks to us today. I will also outline how to interpret the revelation that we receive from God and provide guidelines on how to minister prophetically in different settings. Practical wisdom and insight on avoiding the snares set for those with prophetic callings are also addressed in later chapters.

Before answering these questions, I will first define the terminology used throughout this book.

WHAT IS PROPHECY?

Paul, in his first letter to the Corinthians, gives a simple definition of prophecy.

> **But everyone who prophesies speaks to men for their strengthening, encouragement and comfort (I Corinthians 14:3 NIV).**

Prophesying is speaking in order to strengthen, encourage, and comfort others. However, prophecy is not just speaking human encouragement; it is speaking divine encouragement. In simple terms, prophecy is "hearing" from God and speaking what you hear in order to build, comfort, or encourage someone. To prophesy, is to hear from God and speak to men.

When I use the word "prophecy" in this book, I am describing receiving and giving a specific "word" to a person or group of people. I am not describing a person standing and giving a general exhortation to a congregation during a lull in a meeting.

Although prophesying to a congregation with an encouragement from Scripture or the heart of God is a valid expression of prophecy, that is not the aim of our training. We are specifically seeking to train believers to ask for, recognize, and interpret specific revelation for the purpose of encouraging, building up, or comforting individuals. These same principles can also assist you in receiving prophetic insight for congregations, cities, and nations as well.

THE DIFFERENT PROPHETIC GIFTS

Prophecy includes the spiritual gifts of a *word of knowledge, word of wisdom, discerning of spirits,* and *the gift of prophecy*. For our training purposes, any revelation received from God and communicated to another person will be considered prophecy or a prophetic word. Distinguishing which gift was manifested will not be addressed in every example, due to limited time and space.

In I Corinthians 12:8-10, Paul lists nine distinct spiritual gifts. Three of these gifts can be considered revelatory in nature. They are a word of knowledge, a word of wisdom, and discerning of spirits. A fourth, the gift of prophecy, along with these three revelation gifts make up "the pro-phetic gifts."

Word of Knowledge

A word of knowledge is a specific fact about a person, place, or event that was not obtained through natural means. It could be someone's name, occupation, birthplace, birthday, details about their past history, or other information about them. It generally contains no directional guidance, just facts of information, hence its name—a word of knowledge.

A scriptural example of a word of knowledge is found in John 4. While His disciples entered the city to buy food, Jesus engaged a Samaritan woman in conversation.

> **He said to her, "Go, call your husband, and come here."**
>
> **The woman answered and said, "I have no husband." Jesus said to her, "You have well said, 'I have no husband,'**
>
> **for you have had five husbands, and the one whom you now have is not your husband; this you have said truly."**
>
> **The woman said to Him, "Sir, I perceive that You are a prophet" (John 4:16-19).**

Jesus, having never met the woman, received a word of knowledge about her life. He reveals her marriage, divorce history, and her current living situation. By this word of knowledge, she recognizes God's grace on Jesus, saying, **"Sir, I perceive that You are a prophet."** Paul outlined this as one vital purpose of the word of knowledge.

> **But if all prophesy, and an unbeliever or an ungifted man enters, he is convicted by all, he is called to account by all;**
>
> **the secrets of his heart are disclosed; and so he will fall on his face and worship God, declaring that God is certainly among you (I Corinthians 14:24-25).**

This is the potential power of one word of knowledge. When Jesus spoke to the Samaritan woman, she recognized God's grace on Jesus. Impacted by this encounter, she went forth as an evangelist to her city. The Samaritan woman not only had an encounter with God, but the entire city came to Jesus as a result of this one word of knowledge (see John 4:28-42).

WORD OF WISDOM

A word of wisdom is a divine revelation of the will, plan, or purpose of God for a specific situation. It differs from a word of knowledge in several ways. A word of wisdom is often directional in nature because it contains prophetic insight on what should be done in a situation. A word of wisdom also may not be as dramatic as a word of knowledge, but it may be more needed because it provides divine insight on what we are supposed to do.

In Acts 27, we find a good example of a word of wisdom operating through Paul. Before sailing on a ship, God had given him an impression that the voyage should not take place because there would be difficulty (verse 10). When the ship encountered trouble, Paul had an angelic visitation and was promised protection for everyone on board (verse 22). When the storm began to threaten their lives, the sailors tried to launch a lifeboat. Paul told them that if they did this, they would not be saved (verses 30-31). They abandoned this plan, and eventually all were saved.

This last revelation, that the sailors must remain on the ship, was a word of wisdom. It was not simply information about what had happened or what would happen; it was a revelation of the plan of God for those sailors. It was a revelation about what they were supposed to do. This is the essence of a word of wisdom.

DISCERNING OF SPIRITS

The word "discern" means "to distinguish between." The word "spirit" can mean any of the following in Scripture: angels, demons, the human spirit, the Holy Spirit, anointings, mantles, or the motivating influence of a person. Discerning of spirits, then, is the ability to recognize and distinguish between different types of spirits and anointings.

Many people have been taught that discerning of spirits is the ability to determine when someone has a demonic problem. This is an aspect of this gift, but it is not the full expression of discerning of spirits. It also can identify spiritual gifts and callings, or function like a word of knowledge in healing, identify angelic activity, the state of someone's heart, or the specific purpose of the Lord's presence in a meeting.

A biblical example of this occurs in Acts 16, where Paul encountered a young girl who seemingly spoke the truth.

> **The same followed Paul and us, and cried, saying, These men are the servants of the most high God, which shew unto us the way of salvation.**

And this did she many days. But Paul, being grieved, turned and said to the spirit, I command thee in the name of Jesus Christ to come out of her. And he came out the same hour (Acts 16:17-18 KJV).

Even though what she said was accurate, Paul discerned that she had a spirit of divination (verse 16). She was not speaking from the Holy Spirit, but by a demonic spirit, even though she was speaking truth. Paul was grieved in his spirit; this was how the gift of discerning of spirits operated in him.

I was sitting across the room from a gentleman, and I began to receive prophetic insight about him through the gift of discerning of spirits. I told him that God had called him to raise up home groups in ministry and that the Lord would give him "big meeting dynamics in small groups." Later, he told me that he was a pastor and had transitioned his congregation into a "cell-based" congregation only thirty days previously. He was profoundly encouraged by this word.

In another situation, some friends were praying for a man who had been diagnosed with a serious infection in his body, but the doctors had been unable to pinpoint the location of the infection. As such, they could only treat it generally and the medications they were using were not effective.

When the group was praying for him, one of them felt an unusual sensation in a particular part of his own body. He mentioned this to the man after they finished praying and told him that he felt the doctors would find the infection in the same place. Later that day, the doctor performed a CAT scan on him and discovered the infection at that precise location in his body.

These are just two examples of discerning of spirits. In chapter three, we will discuss further how this gift functions and how it is received and recognized by different people.

PROPHETIC COMPONENTS

Each prophetic word is basically comprised of three different components. These components are the revelation, the interpretation, and the application. Each of these is often a distinct ingredient, but they blend together to comprise a prophetic word.

1) Revelation

The first part of a prophetic word is the information that we receive from God. This is the information that God gives without us having any prior natural understanding. Revelation is basically knowledge or information we could not have known unless God revealed it to us. Revelation comes in varied forms and on different levels.

Revelation can come as a dream, a vision, an impression, or a knowing. It is basically the: "What did you see, hear, or receive?" portion of a prophetic word. It is often useless without an interpretation.

2) Interpretation

The second component of a prophetic word is the interpretation. This is the understanding that God gives about the revelation we have received. Interpretation is the: "What is God saying?" or "What does this mean?" portion of prophecy.

3) Application

The third component of a prophetic word is the application. This is the understanding of how we implement or utilize the revelation and interpretation that we received. Application is the: "What do we do with this?" portion of prophecy. Many times, the application is not our job. Rather, it is left to the person receiving the word to determine what he or she is supposed to do as a result of the prophetic word.

PROPHETIC MINISTRY

Throughout this book, the term "prophetic ministry" is used to describe any time God uses someone to speak or minister prophetically. Any ministry which is prophetic in origin will be called prophetic ministry. In this book, the term does not denote any particular level of prophetic development.

THE PROPHETIC OFFICE

This manual does not deal with the ministry office of the New Testament prophet. The guidelines in this book are parameters for the function of prophecy in the lives of local churches and believers. Although some are relevant, these guidelines should not be misconstrued as guidelines for the function of prophets.

PROPHETIC PEOPLE

This simple designation is used throughout this book to describe anyone with a prophetic calling on his or her life. In our congregations, we currently have approximately five hundred people who are trained to minister prophetically in teams. Of these, probably half have some level of a "prophetic calling" on their lives. The others may be called to teach, pastor, or function in evangelism, or the ministry of helps. Again, this term is not synonymous with the office of a prophet.

Let's Move On

In this chapter, I have provided only the most basic definitions of the different prophetic gifts. They will become clearer as we continue. Now that we have established operational definitions for terms used throughout this book, let's establish a biblical foundation for understanding and receiving the prophetic gifts.

Chapter Two
PROPHETIC MYTHS AND FALLACIES

There are many issues that keep people from functioning in prophetic ministry. Ignorance and apathy are two of the most prevalent. However, there are some concepts and teachings about prophecy and spiritual gifts in general that are worse than ignorance. These wrong concepts have kept multitudes from being equipped for ministry.

We all possess our own theologies concerning spiritual gifts, although most of us could not articulate them. Sadly, our theologies generally have been fashioned more by myths, idealism, and human wisdom than by Scripture. These man-made theologies are often the main stumbling blocks to our functioning in the spiritual gifts which God has made available to us. As such, they must be exposed as the myths and fallacies they are.

To remove these stumbling blocks and discover an accurate foundation for receiving and functioning in the prophetic gifts, we need to examine God's Word. The Bible is our **"more sure word of prophecy" (see II Peter 1:19 KJV)** and provides the only solid foundation for our theology in any area.

THE CREATION OF MYTHS

In general, the myths and fallacies about prophecy and spiritual gifts were created by caring church leaders in reaction to the mistakes of the spiritually immature. Recognizing this, we should understand that these teachings were noble attempts to bring correction in specific, localized situations. While they may have accomplished that purpose, their enduring legacy is that they have kept multitudes from experiencing and walking in the spiritual gifts God has provided for the church.

In this chapter, five basic myths are addressed and compared with scriptural concepts and examples. Although the truths presented are biblical and balanced, they may initially appear extreme. In our idealism, we have allowed human reasoning, instead of God's wisdom, to define much of our Christianity. As a result, we may often have difficulty in recognizing God's ways.

Myth 1: We do not need the gifts of the Spirit; what we really need is the fruit of the Spirit!

While this concept may sound balanced, it is biblically inaccurate. Generally, this teaching has been offered by some in an attempt to bring correction to those who were perceived to pursue spiritual power above righteous character. While seeking spiritual gifts without cultivating spiritual fruit is an error, we should not attempt to correct it by denigrating the importance of spiritual gifts. By attempting to correct one error, we have created another which may be even more destructive.

This teaching also belies a subtle form of pride that implies we do not need spiritual gifts. On the contrary, we desperately need spiritual power to manifest God's kingdom. Our society will not be transformed without the power of God displayed through the church, and spiritual gifts are vital to this process.

One issue that perpetuates the myth that spiritual gifts are optional is an unfortunate translation of the word *charismata*. Most translations have rendered this word as "spiritual gift." To many people, the word "gift" brings to mind something frivolous or fun, but not necessarily useful. A better rendering of *charismata* would be "spiritual enablements" or "spiritual empowerments." In fact, the Amplified Bible uses these two designations for spiritual gifts.

When we understand that spiritual gifts are empowerments provided by God to manifest His kingdom, our attitude toward them will change. No longer will they be seen as optional. Words of knowledge, words of wisdom, and discerning of spirits are gifts in the same way that guns, ammunition, and grenades are gifts for a soldier. They are divine empowerments to operate in the supernatural revelation and power of God.

PAUL'S THEOLOGY

Paul understood the necessity of spiritual gifts. In fact, they provided a key to the fruitfulness of his ministry. When Paul depended on his natural human abilities, the fruit of his ministry was meager. When he depended on God and functioned in spiritual gifts, his ministry was powerful and successful.

At the beginning of his first letter to the Corinthians, Paul makes this comment:

I thank my God always concerning you, for the grace of God which was given you in Christ Jesus,

that in everything you were enriched in Him, in all speech and all knowledge,

19

>even as the testimony concerning Christ
>was confirmed in you,

>so that you are not lacking in any gift . . .
>(I Corinthians 1:4-7).

Paul said his testimony about Christ was proven in the
Corinthians by the fact that they functioned in spiritual
gifts. In other words, the effectiveness of his gospel was
attested by the Corinthians operating in the power of God.
What was Paul's testimony concerning Christ to those in
Corinth?

>**And when I came to you, brethren, I did not
>come with superiority of speech or of wisdom,
>proclaiming to you the testimony of God.**

>**For I determined to know nothing among
>you except Jesus Christ, and Him crucified.**

>**And I was with you in weakness and in fear
>and in much trembling.**

>**And my message and my preaching were not
>in persuasive words of wisdom, but in demon-
>stration of the Spirit and of power,**

>**that your faith should not rest on the wisdom
>of men, but on the power of God (I Corinthians
>2:1-5).**

His testimony concerning Christ was with power and
demonstration of the Spirit, not words of human wisdom.
Paul determined to minister in this way due to his lack of
success in Athens immediately prior to coming to Corinth.
When Paul preached in Athens, he had limited results
because he relied on his own intellect and ability to reason
(see Acts 17:22-18:1).

Since his human wisdom and intellect proved to be of little effect in Athens, Paul purposed not to replicate this mistake in Corinth (see I Corinthians 2:15). Instead, he declared the simple gospel and demonstrated the supernatural power of the Holy Spirit through spiritual gifts, successfully birthing the Corinthian church.

Isn't it time that we made this adjustment as well? Much of the Western church in our generation has depended on eloquence and intellectualism over the power of God. As a result, we have churches whose testimonies reflect human intellect with no supernatural power. Is it possible that if the body of Christ was moving in the spiritual gifts, especially prophecy, the world would not be seeking answers from psychologists and psychics but from the church?

We do not need the fruit of the Spirit instead of the gifts of the Spirit. We need both functioning together in our lives.

MYTH 2: SEEK THE GIVER, NOT THE GIFTS.

Related to the first myth is the idea that we should not seek spiritual gifts, but seek God only. While this makes for a great sermon title, it is also biblically inaccurate. We do need to seek God; however, we should hunger for spiritual gifts as well. Remember, they are not just "gifts." These are the divine enablements to manifest the supernatural power of God as a witness of the gospel.

In another sense, if we reject the gifts God has for us, we are in some fashion rejecting Him. He has given spiritual gifts because they are a manifestation of Himself in our midst.

Thou hast ascended on high, thou hast led captivity captive: thou hast received gifts for

21

men; yea, for the rebellious also, that the LORD
God might dwell among them (Psalm 68:18 KJV).

God has provided these spiritual enablements for us
to receive and demonstrate His supernatural power in
healing, miracles, and prophecy. The church and the world
are desperate for God to make Himself known and dwell
among us. We will not stand in the perilous times ahead,
nor fulfill our mandate in the world without functioning
in all of the spiritual enablements available to us.

"ZEALOUSLY LUST"

Consider Paul's first letter to the Corinthians. First, he
states that the Corinthians are not lacking in any spiritual
gift (see I Corinthians 1:7). Then in I Corinthians 12, he
proceeds to instruct them about the gifts and the function
of the gifts in corporate meetings. Next, he makes this
statement:

But covet earnestly the best gifts: and yet
show I unto you a more excellent way (I Corinthians 12:31 KJV).

To understand the importance of this statement, we
must understand the background of Paul's letter to the
Corinthians. They were already functioning in spiritual
gifts to the degree that when they met as a group, everyone had a revelation, prophecy, song, or a tongue (see I
Corinthians 14:26). However, the gifts were often expressed
without building up the church. People were prophesying
at the same time and speaking messages in other tongues
without anyone interpreting. The gifts were operative, but
presented with little wisdom or order.

To bring balance, Paul, a mature apostle, offers instruction about the gifts and wisdom for administrating their

function in corporate meetings. But he never instructs the Corinthians not to seek spiritual gifts, nor criticizes them for being too focused on spiritual gifts. On the contrary, he urges the Corinthians, who are already moving fluently in spiritual gifts, to "earnestly covet" them. Upon further study, I discovered that this same Greek word translated "earnestly covet" can also be translated as "zealously lust"!

Immediately after encouraging them to zealously lust after spiritual gifts, Paul launches into a profound discourse on the proper motivating influence and overriding manner in which the gifts are to be administered, which is love. Again, many have misunderstood this passage as communicating that we should be seeking love and leave off hungering for spiritual enablements. But this is inaccurate. Paul is imploring the Corinthians to function in spiritual gifts out of a heart of love for one another and in a loving manner.

In the first verse after his exhortation on love, Paul again implores the Corinthians to pursue love and to zealously lust after spiritual gifts, especially prophecy (see I Corinthians 14:1). So, surrounding our pursuit of love on both sides should be a zealous lust for spiritual enablements.

"JACOB HAVE I LOVED"

Several years ago, I was complaining to the Lord about some of the strange people who come to our ministry because of our prophetic reputation. People have arrived at our congregation and declared that God was going to "take us home" and give them our mantle for ministry. As I was telling the Lord how much I hated that kind of behavior, He spoke these words very clearly to me: *I don't hate that Steve; I love that kind of heart.* I was stunned. Then the Lord quoted this Scripture to me: **"Jacob have I loved, but Esau have I hated" (see Romans 9:13 KJV).**

How could God love Jacob? Jacob lusted after the birthright that belonged to his brother. The biblical birthright represented spiritual blessing and authority. Jacob was so consumed with the desire to have spiritual blessing and authority that he was willing to deceive his own family to obtain it! How could God love someone who was so blinded by his lust for spiritual blessing and authority that he was willing to deceive his father to get it?

This is offensive to our human ideas of proper behavior and motivation. But while it may offend us, God loves this kind of heart. God says that He loves those who so hunger for His power, presence, and authority that they are willing to do anything to get it. **"Jacob have I *loved*."**

The Scripture could have read, "Israel have I loved." But God said that He loved Jacob, using the name indicative of the lusting, deceiving man that Jacob was prior to his nature being changed. While we may judge those who hunger for God's power and authority as being extreme and unbalanced, God may be more pleased with them than with those who appear humanly righteous, but who, like Esau, are complacent toward spiritual matters.

Not only does Scripture say that God loved Jacob, it also says that He hated Esau. There is no other record in Scripture of God hating someone. Esau was so preoccupied with the natural realm that he despised spiritual things. In our human reasoning, we esteem those who are conservative, balanced, and proper. God has a different standard. He hates the attitude of those who do not esteem His power, presence, or blessings as being worthy of their attention.

From the time of man's creation, God has desired to share His nature, glory, and power. This was His original intention. He has longed for those who would so hunger and thirst for His power, presence, anointing, authority, and blessing that they would pursue Him for it. Too many generations have been like Esau, despising the richness of God's blessing, and setting their hearts on temporary things, forfeiting the opportunity to share in His glory and power.

If we want to obtain all that the Lord has for us and others, we must have the attitude of Jacob. Just as with Jacob, God will confront and deal with our character issues, but we must pursue the spiritual authority and blessings He has for us. These blessings include the spiritual enablements God has provided for us to manifest His supernatural power.

Myth 3: Seeking Spiritual Gifts Is Selfish.

Another aspect of the "Seek the Giver of the gifts" teaching suggests that having a desire for spiritual gifts is selfish. Again, while some will always have questionable motives, this concept is inaccurate since spiritual enablements are given in order to minister to others. Serving others is not selfish; it is the essence of ministry. Of course, it is possible to possess a desire to minister that includes mixed motives. However, we should not react to the bad motives of a few individuals and create teachings that equate a desire for spiritual enablements with the desire for recognition.

Again, consider the attitude of Paul toward those who were ministering from questionable motives.

It is true that some preach Christ out of envy and rivalry...

...out of selfish ambition, not sincerely, supposing that they can stir up trouble for me while I am in chains.

But what does it matter? The important thing is that in every way, whether from false motives or true, Christ is preached. And because of this I rejoice. Yes, and I will continue to rejoice (Philippians 1:15, 17-18 NIV).

Paul was not reactionary simply because some were motivated by selfish ambition, envy, and jealousy. On the contrary, he rejoiced that the gospel was being preached. Likewise, we should rejoice when people are pursuing God or spiritual enablements, because the majority of the church is Laodicean in nature—focusing on the temporary and being self-satisfied.

Paul never discouraged the Corinthians from hungering after spiritual enablements. Rather, he implored them to zealously lust after them. To establish order in the Corinthian church, he expounded on the proper motivation for functioning in spiritual gifts (love) and the correct order for functioning in the gifts during public gatherings. He never discouraged anyone from hungering after spiritual gifts and neither should we.

Myth 4: Asking for Spiritual Gifts Opens Us to Demonic Deception.

Some have proposed that a person asking the Lord for a dream, vision, or word can instead receive demonic visions or satanic revelations. This teaching has effectively stopped multitudes from asking God for spiritual gifts, and it has been an accepted teaching in some circles for years.

Whenever I speak at a conference, I usually ask how many people have heard this teaching and believed it. Generally, about 25 to 50 percent of the people acknowledge having been taught this, even though it is not found anywhere in Scripture. Not only is there no scriptural basis for this concept, but it is a direct contradiction to Jesus' teaching in the Gospels.

> **And he said unto them, Which of you shall have a friend, and shall go unto him at midnight, and say unto him, Friend, lend me three loaves;**
>
> **For a friend of mine in his journey is come to me, and I have nothing to set before him?**
>
> **And he from within shall answer and say, Trouble me not: the door is now shut, and my children are with me in bed; I cannot rise and give thee.**
>
> **I say unto you, Though he will not rise and give him, because he is his friend, yet because of his importunity he will rise and give him as many as he needeth.**
>
> **And I say unto you, Ask, and it shall be given you; seek, and ye shall find; knock, and it shall be opened unto you.**
>
> **For every one that asketh receiveth; and he that seeketh findeth; and to him that knocketh it shall be opened.**
>
> **If a son shall ask bread of any of you that is a father, will he give him a stone? or if he ask a fish, will he for a fish give him a serpent?**

Or if he shall ask an egg, will he offer him a scorpion?

If ye then, being evil, know how to give good gifts unto your children: how much more shall your heavenly Father give the Holy Spirit to them that ask him? (Luke 11:5-13 KJV)

In this parable, Jesus told about a man who asked for bread from his friend so that he could feed someone who was passing by on a journey. He said the friend would not give bread to the man simply because he was a friend, but because the man continued to ask. He also said the neighbor would give to his friend as much as he needed for the person on the journey. While pondering this Scripture, I realized that Jesus was describing us perfectly when we ask for a "prophetic word" for those who need to hear from God.

We all have people who cross our paths on their journey of life and need desperately to hear from God. But we realize that we have nothing to give them because our human wisdom is insufficient for their need. If we will go to our Friend (Jesus), and ask Him for bread (a word of knowledge, word of wisdom, or prophetic insight) to give to this person, He will give us as much as we need to feed this person (minister to them).

Jesus then dispels the myth that in asking Him for a word to help others, we must beware of receiving something harmful or damaging to us. He specifically uses symbolism identified with demonic things to clearly establish this truth. He said that if we ask for bread, fish, or eggs (things that nourish and feed) He would not give us stones, serpents, or scorpions (demonic things).

Why would God implore us to ask and keep on asking, seek and keep on seeking, knock and keep on knocking for a word for someone, and then allow us to receive something demonic instead? He would not do this! If we give good "gifts" to our children, why would we think that God is less righteous than we? He is the perfect Father, and He encourages us to seek Him for power and ability in order to minister to others.

We can trust in the goodness of our heavenly Father. Jesus has promised us that when we ask for the Holy Spirit and His gifts, we will not receive anything evil. On the contrary, He knows how to give good gifts to those who ask Him.

Myth 5: Only a Few Special People Are Called to Prophesy.

In his discourse to the Corinthians, Paul clearly speaks to this issue.

> **For ye may all prophesy one by one, that all may learn, and all may be comforted (I Corinthians 14:31 KJV).**

Paul stated that all may prophesy. Jesus said that His sheep hear His voice. As stated before, prophecy in its most basic form is hearing what God is saying about someone and relaying it to them. If all believers can hear His voice, then all can prophesy. If you are born again, you can prophesy. You may need to develop your sensitivity and understanding of what God is saying, but you have the ability and potential to prophesy. It is not limited to special people.

Although we may all acknowledge this Scripture as true and mentally assent to it, we have a harder time believing it. Most of us begin to ascribe special status to a person who becomes proficient in any spiritual gift. We tend to see that person as special because he or she can do something special in spiritual matters.

As we do this, we begin to be hindered from believing that God can do the same things through us, because most of us do not believe that we are in the "special" category.

We should remember, however, that God does not usually choose people because they are special or gifted. In fact, Paul states just the opposite concerning most who are called of God.

> **For consider your calling, brethren, that there were not many wise according to the flesh, not many mighty, not many noble;**

> **but God has chosen the foolish things of the world to shame the wise, and God has chosen the weak things of the world to shame the things which are strong,**

> **and the base things of the world and the despised, God has chosen, the things that are not, that He might nullify the things that are,**

> **that no man should boast before God.**

> **But by His doing you are in Christ Jesus, who became to us wisdom from God, and righteousness and sanctification, and redemption (I Corinthians 1:26-30).**

Anyone who consistently prophesies has simply been gifted by God and has developed that gift by using it. The fact that we are so quick to ascribe the ability as being inherent in the person shows how much we still trust in the flesh instead of God. Trusting in the flesh includes trusting in any human abilities, whether in us or in others.

Instead, we should take great encouragement when anyone begins to move proficiently in spiritual gifts, knowing that they are not special in and of themselves, but that God has gifted them. If we understand this, we will be confident that God will use us also.

THE "OX STALL" PRINCIPLE

A general motivating factor behind most of these teachings is an aversion to mistakes and a misunderstanding of God's ways. Whereas most of us tend to honor neatness and order, God prefers life, and life is generally not too orderly. Having assisted in the delivery of each of my children, I can attest that life begins with a mess. Because we have not understood how truly organic spiritual things are, the church has missed much of what God has for us. **"Where no oxen are, the manger is clean, but much increase comes by the strength of the ox" (Proverbs 14:4).**

If we want increase in the church, it will come with a price. The cost of increase in the kingdom of God is a messy stall, but there is no other valid option. Our focus must begin to change from an honoring of order to an honoring of life. We must begin to discover God's ways and participate with Him, and not create stumbling blocks through our reactions.

THE DANGER OF SAFETY

There is an inherent danger in our attempts to make walking with God safer than He has made it. If we become overly focused on the extremes and mistakes of a small minority in order to establish safety for others, we will formulate teachings that cause people to become eccentric or off centered. Those who consistently sit under teachings designed to correct extremes will eventually become extreme themselves—extremely cautious and fearful of mistakes. This perspective is exactly the opposite of the faith required to walk with God.

There will always be mistakes. There were mistakes made by the greatest leaders in the early church, including Jesus' disciples. As long as God works through fallen men in this present age, we will witness mistakes and errors. If we lose sight of this and become reactionary in our teachings, we make the biggest mistake of all by creating stumbling blocks that hinder us from God's provision.

While we must not overreact to mistakes, we cannot ignore them either. We must learn from them and grow into maturity. However, we cannot propagate teachings that appear to be balanced, but which are contrary to God and His plan. God's ways are not our ways, and His thoughts are not our thoughts (see Isaiah 55:8).

BE ENCOURAGED

Earlier in my Christian walk, I was quite reactionary. In fact, I believed and taught all five of the myths previously listed, but I eventually discovered that they were contrary to God's ways. When God changed my understanding, I changed my teachings, and the results have been amazing.

In the last four years, we have seen thousands of believers who have never moved in prophetic gifts begin to prophesy accurately with minimal training. We have found that most Christians are already hearing God's voice, but they have been hindered through a lack of instruction or through some of these reactionary teachings.

The primary way that we have seen so many released is by removing the lies that bind them through sound biblical instruction. We provide basic instruction in recognizing how God is speaking to them as individuals and then give them an opportunity to begin ministering with their spiritual gifts. We also provide scriptural parameters within which they can minister, creating an atmosphere of safety for both them and those receiving ministry.

As people have been freed from the hindrances placed upon them by reactionary teachings, they have begun to move more powerfully in ministry than they thought possible. We have received thousands of testimonies from people whose lives have been changed through a word given by those who have only been ministering in prophecy a short time. The mistakes and errors that we have seen are minuscule compared to the fruit that has come from the prophetic ministry. God's ways are better than our own.

We must be freed from artificial restraints so that we can be yoked with the Lord in ministry. As we are freed from the lies that bind us, we will begin to learn of Him and be used by Him in amazing ways. He is well able to bring correction to us in His manner and in the proper time as His nature and power are revealed in us.

Chapter Three

HOW GOD SPEAKS

God often chooses to speak in strange ways and through unusual means. This is one of the primary reasons why many people do not recognize when God is speaking to them. As we examine how God speaks, let us remember that He is the Creator and that His creativity is expressed in the ways He communicates. In fact, we must recognize that God's voice is seldom really a "voice."

THE VOICE OF GOD

In John 1:1, Jesus is called the **"Word of God."** Aside from theological implications, this description reveals that God is a communicator. He is the Word, and He created all things with the word of His mouth (see Genesis 1; Hebrews 1:2). In the Garden, Adam heard the sound of **"God's voice"** walking in the cool of the day as He sought fellowship with the man and the woman (see Genesis 3:8). Fundamental to God's nature is that He is a communicator.

In the same way, fundamental to every believer's nature is the ability to hear God's voice. If you are a Christian, you have already heard God speak. In fact, you cannot come to Jesus unless the Father draws you. You must "hear His voice" in order to be drawn to Him. Although you probably did not literally hear a voice tell you that Jesus was the Son of God, somehow you realized that the gospel was true. In essence, you were led by the Father to the Son.

"No one can come to Me unless the Father who sent Me draws him; and I will raise him up on the last day.

"It is written in the prophets, 'And they shall all be taught of God.' Everyone who has heard and learned from the Father, comes to Me" (John 6:44-45).

When I minister in prophetic training seminars, I routinely ask how many of those in attendance are consistently hearing God speak. Generally about 10 percent of the people acknowledge that they hear from God consistently. After the conference, virtually everyone understands that God has been speaking to them all along; they have simply failed to recognize it.

The goal of this chapter is to help you recognize how God speaks so that you can recognize when He speaks to you for others. Keep in mind that this book is not intended as a primer on receiving personal guidance from God, but instead is designed to help equip you to function prophetically, which is hearing from God for others and speaking those words to them.

Ways and Means

God communicates in strange ways for a variety of reasons, which we will explore later. Presently, we only need to understand the different ways He speaks.

He said, "Hear now My words: If there is a prophet among you, I, the LORD, shall make Myself known to him in a vision. I shall speak with him in a dream.

"Not so, with My servant Moses, He is faithful in all My household;

"With him I speak mouth to mouth, even openly, and not in dark sayings..." (Numbers 12:6-8).

Job 33:14-17 also outlines these same ways in which God speaks. Dreams, visions, and dark sayings are fundamental ways in which God speaks. The word translated **"dark sayings"** (see Psalm 78:2) here means a riddle or puzzle. God often speaks in riddles or parables which require us to do some research in order to discover what He is saying.

In chapter one, we identified the spiritual enablements that are considered "prophetic gifts." In this chapter, we will discuss the different ways in which God gives us words of knowledge, words of wisdom, discerning of spirits, and prophecy. But first we need to understand that there are different levels of prophetic revelation.

LEVELS OF REVELATION

Some types of revelation are of a higher order than others. The reason for understanding the different levels of revelation will become apparent later as we discuss administrating prophecy. For now, we simply need to acknowledge the different levels.

Lower levels of revelation include mental or spiritual impressions or perceptions, gentle internal visions, and the still, small voice of God that we hear in our spirits. Each of these is a valid type of revelation, albeit lower level.

Higher level revelations include open visions, angelic visitations, visitations of the Lord, vivid dreams, trances, being caught up in the Spirit, and other prophetic experiences. As a general rule, the less subjective way in which a revelation comes, the higher level it is.

PROPHETIC IMPRESSIONS—PART I

Impressions are the most simple form of prophetic revelation. Almost every Christian is hearing God speak through impressions. But because of general ignorance about revelation gifts in the church, many do not recognize these impressions as God-given, but discount them as stray thoughts or coincidence.

Most people have experienced the phenomenon of suddenly thinking about someone they have not seen or heard from in years, then "by chance" encountering that person later that same day or week. Others, during the course of their day, have a "stray thought" about something a friend or acquaintance needs to do. Later, it is discovered that their stray thought was an accurate insight.

What many people think are coincidences are actually valid prophetic impressions from God. What would happen if you began recognizing the impressions you receive as being from God? He would begin using you to speak to people that He wants to touch.

A CONTEMPORARY EXAMPLE

While driving to an appointment and thinking about nothing in particular, this thought passed through my mind: *It's time for Bill to leave his job and begin pastoring that congregation in South Carolina full-time.* Since I had not been thinking about Bill, I recognized this "passing thought" as an impression from the Lord. Grabbing my Day-Timer, I made a quick note to call Bill when I returned to my office.

When I arrived back at the office, I found that Bill had called at precisely the moment I received this impression. When I returned his call, his first statement to me was, "Is it time for me to leave my job and pastor this church full-time?" I told him about the impression and the timing of it. He immediately left secular employment and began pastoring full-time. His decision has born significant fruit in his life and in the congregation he serves.

What came as an impression or stray thought was the specific answer from God that Bill needed. This word gave him the confidence that this choice was in accordance with God's will and timing. He needed that assurance to endure the difficulties that would arise from launching into this transition.

It is virtually impossible to overestimate the value of a single prophetic revelation. God wants to encourage, build up, and comfort the people surrounding us. As we learn to recognize and understand the different ways in which God speaks to us, He can use us in ways we may never have imagined.

SCRIPTURAL EXAMPLES OF IMPRESSIONS

The Bible contains several powerful examples of impression-level revelations. In Acts 14:9, Paul perceived that a man who was crippled from birth had faith for healing. When Paul acted on his impression, the man was dramatically healed. Paul did not receive a high level revelation such as an audible voice or a vision, but simply had a perception or impression!

As another example, Paul also had a prophetic impression while being transported to Rome for trial. **"Sirs, I perceive that this voyage will be with hurt and much damage, not only of the lading and ship, but also of our lives" (Acts 27:10 KJV).** Later, the Lord spoke more clearly to Paul and he received a higher level revelation concerning what would transpire, along with a word of wisdom for keeping everyone safe (see Acts 27:22-25).

Impressions are the entry-level prophetic revelation for most people, but this does not imply that impressions are not significant. Paul, a mature apostle, continued to receive insight and help from God through prophetic impressions throughout his ministry. Today, many seasoned prophetic ministers also continue to receive impression-level revelation, even though God frequently speaks to them through higher level revelation.

Prophetic Impressions—Part 2

In addition to impressions perceived by the mind or spirit, God also speaks through impressions in our bodies. Many people receive words of knowledge for healing in this way. God will allow us to feel a sensation or impression in our body which reveals someone else's injury or sickness. While praying for someone, we may begin to feel an unusual sensation in our body which was not present prior to praying. This is God identifying a specific condition that needs healing. We can then speak this word of knowledge to them and minister healing as their faith is heightened.

Vicki was praying for a woman and began to feel pain in her own hands. When Vicki asked the woman if she suffered pain in her hands, she confirmed that she was currently in great pain. They prayed together for healing and the woman experienced immediate relief.

Marla received an impression in her body, not while praying, but just in her daily routine and was able to minister with power as a result. As she walked into a place of business, she suddenly noticed a burning sensation on her right forearm. When she asked if anyone was experiencing pain on the inside of their right forearm, a young lady passing through the office rolled up her right sleeve.

Two days before, she had burned her arm in the identical place where Marla had received the impression in her own body. They prayed and God removed all of her pain as new skin began to miraculously appear over the burned place while many people in the office watched.

These are only two of literally thousands of examples that our teams have received over the past five years. Receiving impressions in our bodies about someone else is a primary way we receive words of knowledge for healing. In one particular meeting, God identified and healed approximately fifty people with vision and eye ailments through a word of knowledge received in this way.

Jesus also received insight from His Father in this fashion. In the Gospel of Luke, Jesus was walking through a city and the people were pressing in and cramming together to touch Him. A woman with an issue of blood believed that if she could touch Him, she would be healed. She pressed through the crowd and touched Him. Jesus immediately knew it, and said,

> **...Who touched me? When all denied, Peter and they that were with him said, Master, the multitude throng thee and press thee, and sayest thou, Who touched me?**

> **And Jesus said, Somebody hath touched me: for I perceive that virtue is gone out of me (Luke 8:45-46 KJV).**

This word translated **"perceive"** means "to know by feeling." Jesus knew that someone had touched Him because He felt in His body that virtue had gone out of Him. It is interesting to note that Jesus did not know who had touched Him. This is true of us as well. Many times, we receive clear impressions about what is happening, but like Marla in the example above, we must use faith and ask who has the ailment. We know in part and we prophesy in part.

PROPHETIC IMPRESSIONS—PART 3

God will also speak to you through impressions in your emotions. Whereas other impressions are informational in nature, these are more emotional in nature or "feeling oriented." Don't be disturbed by this description. Although our feelings are often inaccurate indicators of reality, God created our emotions and will sometimes speak to us through them for others.

Many times God will allow us to feel in our own soul what someone else is experiencing. We might feel a grief or a sorrow as we pray for someone in a meeting or for a waitress at a restaurant. God is allowing us to feel what they are feeling so we can minister to them. As we recognize and identify these prophetic feelings, we can see people healed and delivered.

At other times, we will feel what the Lord feels for someone to whom we are ministering. We may experience profound joy or a sense of protection over a person we hardly know. We can prophesy to them that God rejoices over them with singing (see Zephaniah 3:17) or that the Lord will keep them as the apple of His eye (see Zechariah 2:8).

A friend of mine was praying with an acquaintance and began to feel a terrible shame come over her own soul. After a moment, she realized that this shame was identical to what she had experienced after having an abortion several years before she met the Lord. As she identified what God was allowing her to feel in her soul, and remembered the reason she had felt such shame years ago, she realized that God was giving her a word of knowledge about this person she was praying for.

My friend began ministering prophetically to this young lady by gently revealing that she knew this girl had turned to drugs and promiscuity because of the pain and shame of having an abortion. This was done privately and in love in order to heal her soul, not to expose her past sin. The girl was stunned by this revelation and wept as God touched her deeply. This young girl was then delivered of her drug addiction and shame.

Many people who receive impressions like this may believe they are unstable because their emotions can change abruptly as they move from one situation to another. They do not understand that God is "pulling the strings on their emotions" in order to speak to them. However, when they understand that these "feelings" are from God, they can become powerful ministers of His grace and mercy.

Wisdom and Balance

While God does speak in this way, we need to recognize a truth. Accurately discerning God's voice in your feelings takes great discipline and wisdom. Obviously not everything that anyone feels is from God. To the degree that we are self-centered or wounded, our feelings will be dangerously inaccurate. This is addressed in greater detail in chapter five.

To guard against this, we must hide God's Word in our hearts. When we do so, the thoughts and emotions of our hearts will be discerned.

> **For the word of God is quick, and powerful, and sharper than any twoedged sword, piercing even to the dividing asunder of soul and spirit, and of the joints and marrow, and is a discerner of the thoughts and intents of the heart (Hebrews 4:12 KJV).**

If we know the Word of God and judge our feelings by it, we will know and discern what is coming from our souls, versus what is coming into our souls from the Spirit of God. We must filter our impressions through the more sure word of prophecy, which is the Bible.

PROPHETIC SENSES

Using the model of our five physical senses—sight, hearing, smell, taste, and touch—we will discover another way that God speaks to us. He will give us revelation through seeing, hearing, smelling, tasting, and touching spiritually. Although this may initially sound strange, there is a scriptural precedent for God speaking to us through our "spiritual senses."

1) Spiritual Sight

Prophets were often called "seers" in the Old Testament. In II Kings 2, we find a biblical example of the gift of discerning of spirits operating through "spiritual sight." When Elijah is translated to heaven, Elisha received a double portion of the spirit that was upon him, and he also received Elijah's mantle for ministry. Consider what the sons of the prophets said when they saw him:

> **Now when the sons of the prophets who were at Jericho opposite him saw him, they said, "The spirit of Elijah rests on Elisha." And they**

came to meet him and bowed themselves to the ground before him (II Kings 2:15).

These young men **"saw"** that the spirit of Elijah was now upon Elisha. What did they see? Was there some physical change in Elisha? Or was it a spiritual change that they could see with their spiritual eyes? There was a spiritual presence that was once upon Elijah, that they now **"saw"** upon Elisha. This was the prophetic mantle or authority in which Elijah had walked.

Often when I meet someone, I will see a similarity in their countenance to someone else I know or know of. But they do not look like this person at all. Rather, the Lord is showing me through *spiritual sight* that there is some aspect of his or her life which is identical to this other person.

Many times, the Lord will reveal that this individual has a similar spiritual calling as the other person. Sometimes they were born in the same state or have the same occupation. In some instances, they have the same name.

When we taught about God speaking through "spiritual sight" in our fellowship, we found that approximately half of the people were receiving revelation from God in this way. However, most of them had never understood what they were seeing and had never prophesied to anyone based on it. Many people who had never given a prophetic word were soon receiving and recognizing revelation and prophesying accurately by "seeing" spiritually.

Donna noticed a man who was visiting our meetings from the Pacific Coast. She realized that something about him reminded her of a cousin whom she had not seen in years. As she related this to her husband, he recognized that God had opened her spiritual eyes to see something. When her husband asked what she thought about when this cousin came to mind, she related some problems he had encountered early in life and how they had affected him throughout his entire life. Donna's husband turned to the man and announced that Donna had received a prophetic word for him.

Donna then shared with this man the specific problems her cousin had encountered and that although this man had endured the same things, God was now enabling him to overcome them. The man was stunned and began weeping as Donna ministered to him because every one of these details was true, and he left the meeting greatly encouraged by the Lord.

Immediately after ministering to this gentleman, Donna realized the man looked nothing like her cousin and she could not even tell by his appearance what had caused her to think that he did. It was obvious that although there was no similarity in their physical appearance, God had opened her spiritual eyes to see something prophetically.

In another example, I was praying for a woman and "saw" her hands as though they were completely white. It was so unusual I immediately asked, "What is this, Lord?" I then realized He wanted her to know that she was blameless and that He saw her as having spotlessly clean hands. She began to weep as God set her free from the enemy's accusations over some things in her past for which she was wrongly blamed.

The examples of receiving revelation in this fashion from just our local prophetic teams are too numerous to list. We have hundreds of testimonies where God has spoken this way and brought healing, deliverance, or confirmation to people. More examples will be included in the next chapter.

2) Spiritual Hearing

Another way God gives revelation is through *spiritual hearing*. Like spiritual sight, God will give us revelation when we hear a person speak or we hear someone speak a name. By spiritual hearing, I do not mean that we hear when people sound depressed or excited because of the tone of their voice; instead we are spiritually discerning this.

One of the first times this happened to me, I was riding with a friend who was a Baptist youth pastor. As he drove, he shared his concern for several of his charges, but one in particular. When he mentioned this young man by name, I answered, "Oh, you mean the redheaded kid." When I said this, the presence of God filled the car as we were stunned by this revelation, knowing that I had never met this young man.

The youth pastor's concern was immediately turned to encouragement, realizing that God specifically knew this young man and was working in his life. He changed his approach to helping this young man whose life soon turned around.

In another instance, while working in our office, I answered a phone call from a woman I had never met, but had only talked to by phone several times. Upon hearing her voice, I knew instantly that she had changed her hairstyle into a more "mature style." When I related this to her, she was stunned and acknowledged changing her hairstyle the previous day. When I asked the Lord what this meant, He said there were certain things she had been praying for which were now coming to maturity in her life. She was stunned since she had been praying for those very things that week.

God will also reveal struggles that people are experiencing, encouragements He has for them, and many other things in this fashion. If we will learn to identify when we hear something unusual and ask the Lord, He will give us a powerful ministry for people.

3) Spiritual Smell

Another unusual way in which God speaks is through the spiritual sense of smell. Just as with sight and hearing, God will often cause us to spiritually smell things that are messages or revelations.

In the early days of MorningStar Publications and Ministries, we were a very small ministry with little resources. My wife and I lived for a time with Rick and Julie Joyner and their two children in a large house we rented, which also housed our offices. Late one evening as I was retiring to bed, I smelled something strange and inquired of the Lord. He told me that a virus had been released from the enemy against us and to rebuke it and pray for protection. I obeyed the Lord and prayed for protection over Angie and me.

The next morning, both Angie and I were fine. But later that day, I discovered that Rick and his family had gotten sick from a virus during the night. In my zeal for my own family, I had forgotten to pray for the Joyners. While I was upset over my mistake (and so was Rick), this did confirm the validity of what I had discerned by smell the previous evening.

God also gives us revelation through smell that confirms His work, not just the enemy's. While ministering once in Switzerland, a friend and I were praying for a young lady and both of us immediately smelled incense. She smelled the incense along with us, but no one else in the ministry situation did, although several others were standing right beside us. We began speaking to her about the presence of the Lord radiating from her life as an incense. She began to weep and rejoice as God healed her wounded heart and confirmed her preciousness to Him. When I saw her several months later, she had blossomed into a powerful woman of God.

4) *Spiritual Touch*

God also speaks to us many times through impressions that come through touching. Often, when I am ministering prophetically in a congregation, God will not speak to me until I lay hands on those for whom I am praying. Often this is because the Lord wants the ministry to be up close and personal. Some people receive revelation concerning specific areas of sickness and disease as they pray while touching an individual. This can also happen in other areas of touch.

An example occurred several years ago when I was walking by a fax machine. A confidential fax had just been received for Rick Joyner, and as I was placing it in his incoming mailbox, I "felt" a control spirit on it. I did not discern this by reading the fax, but rather by touching it. Later, when I talked with Rick, I mentioned this impression to him. He was stunned. He had been asking the Lord for insight as to how to deal appropriately with this fax that had troubled him.

How did I discern a control spirit behind the message in this fax? When I touched the fax paper, I felt in my soul what I feel when someone tries to control or manipulate me. I had learned to recognize this by being on the receiving end of manipulation and control in years past. God has redeemed those situations by using my remembrance of that feeling for His purpose of discernment.

5) *Spiritual Taste*

This is similar in nature and application to receiving revelation through spiritual smell. Several times while praying for individuals, I have suddenly had a very distinct taste in my mouth that was not there previously. When I inquired of the Lord, I realized these tastes were actually prophetic revelation concerning those to whom I was ministering. I was then able to prophesy to them. Others experience this phenomenon when praying for those who are sick.

I realize that some of these phenomena may seem strange, but compared to the biblical record, they are relatively innocuous. We need to consider that Jesus healed people by spitting on their tongue, spitting on their eyes, or putting mud in their eyes. Remember, if we are to read the Scriptures honestly, we must conclude by agreeing with God's Word to Isaiah: **"For my thoughts are not your thoughts, neither are your ways my ways, saith the LORD" (Isaiah 55:8 KJV).**

God's ways are not our ways and guess whose ways must change? In order to hear Him speak, we must be open to the different and unusual ways He chooses to communicate with us. He often chooses weak, base, and foolish things to confound the wisdom of the wise, and often we must be willing to become foolish in order to hear Him (see I Corinthians 1:27).

The Voice of the Lord

God does speak to us in plain words at times. In general, when we talk about God speaking to us, we mean God has communicated with us through an impression, vision, or some other means. However, we must not lose sight of the fact that He also simply "speaks" to us by His voice.

But even within hearing the voice of the Lord, there are different levels of revelation and different ways in which He speaks. I have listed the most common. While I have not provided clear Scripture for these different designations, Scripture does mention the "still, small voice," and God speaking audibly at times. Some of the designations we make here are simply descriptive in nature.

1) Still, Small Voice of God

This is a lower level revelation for the most part and probably all Christians have heard the Lord speak to them in this fashion. This is the soft and gentle voice of God which comes as we wait on the Lord in prayer or meditation. God speaks this way for personal instruction or encouragement. It is a highly subjective way to hear God, since it comes internally and quietly. It is a valid way that God speaks, but it must be judged in light of the desires of our own hearts (see chapter eleven for more details).

2) Internal, Audible Voice of God

This is a higher level revelation than the still, small voice because it is less subjective in nature. This is often a loud, booming voice, not coming in our thoughts, but instead cutting through and interrupting them. Although this is not really audible, it seems to be because it resounds so loudly within us.

Matt, one of our pastors, was standing on the platform as we ministered prophetically during a conference. While looking over the crowd of eight hundred people and asking the Lord to speak, Matt's eyes fell on a couple sitting in the middle of the room. He could only see them from their shoulders up. When he saw them, he heard the Lord say (internally, but loud) "The baby is okay." Matt then called them out and said "I believe the Lord wants you to know that the baby is okay." They both smiled and acknowledged the word.

We then asked them to stand and tell us what this meant to them. As the woman stood up, everyone saw that she was about seven months pregnant. They related to everyone present that they had begun to have some concern about their unborn child and had asked God to confirm that the baby was okay. They contacted us when the baby was born to give us the report that their baby was perfect.

3) Audible Voice of God

This is obviously a higher level of revelation than hearing God speak internally. The audible voice of God is difficult to describe, except to say if you only *think* you have heard God speak audibly, you have not. When He speaks in this fashion, all thought and doubt is removed. It is not so much that it is loud in volume, but that it is immense in nature.

The first three times I heard the audible voice of the Father, it was like hearing eternity speak, and I was shaken for weeks afterward. There is no mistaking the audible voice of God. It is a very high level revelation, though it may still need interpretation as well. God does not frequently speak in this fashion.

THE PUN IS MIGHTIER THAN THE SWORD

Believe it or not, God will often use puns or plays on words when He speaks to us. This may be difficult to accept, even with many contemporary examples, but this manner of speaking is also established in Scripture.

> **And the word of the LORD came to me saying, "What do you see, Jeremiah?" And I said, "I see a rod of an almond tree."**

> **Then the LORD said to me, "You have seen well, for I am watching over My word to perform it" (Jeremiah 1:11-12).**

What did the Lord mean when He said, **"You have seen well, for I am watching over My word to perform it."** What did that have to do with Jeremiah seeing the rod of an almond tree? Since most of us do not read the Bible in Hebrew, we do not understand this exchange between God and Jeremiah. If we could read this in Hebrew, we would recognize this as a play on words or a pun.

When the Lord asked Jeremiah what he saw, he answered, *"shawkade"* which means an "almond tree." The Lord replies to him, "You have seen well, for I will *'shawkad'"* which means "watch over My word to perform it." God uses the similarity between the two words to speak to Jeremiah about how He is watching over His Word to bring it to pass. In the same way, God will use puns or plays on words to speak to us today.

VISIONS

There are many different ways in which God speaks to us, which are included under the general category of *visions*.

There are *glimpses in the Spirit, gentle internal visions, strong internal visions,* and *open visions*. These are described below.

We must remember that God not only spoke in visions to the Old Covenant saints, but He did this with the New Testament believers as well. He continues to speak this way to many today. Personally, I see glimpses and visions almost continually when praying for people.

On the scale of prophetic revelation, visions are generally a higher level of revelation than impressions because they are less subjective in nature than impressions. Listed below are a few details and examples of the different types of visions. We will deal more with visions as we discuss interpretation in chapter four.

1) Glimpses in the Spirit

These are the lowest level of visions and are fleeting internal pictures that we receive from the Lord. They are brief in duration and usually contain only a still picture, not a scene or a story line. Although a lower form of revelation, God can speak powerfully through these gentle visions.

Many of these glimpses are symbolic in nature also. When praying for people, I often see glimpses or still pictures in my spirit that mean nothing to me initially. I then will have to pray for an interpretation in order to understand what God is saying.

2) Gentle Internal Visions and Strong, Internal Visions

Internal visions are much stronger than simple glimpses although they are still "seen" internally. As a rule, these visions are more than just still pictures; they include a "story line" of transpiring events. This type of vision can be interrupted by distractions, and good focus is needed to

54

keep from missing them. Since strong, internal visions are clearer and more pronounced than gentle internal visions, they are a higher level of revelation.

By listing both gentle and strong internal visions, I have acknowledged that some internal visions are decidedly stronger than others. The key point is that the strong internal visions are a higher level of revelation than the more gentle ones.

3) Open Visions

These are a considerably higher level revelation than impressions, internal visions, or the internal voice of God. These visions are received when your eyes are open and are not stopped by distractions. These visions can start and continue even when you are involved in an attention consuming activity, such as driving a car. The experience is similar to seeing a scene acted out physically as on a movie screen.

Open visions are a higher level of revelation than internal visions, again because they are less subjective in nature. While an internal vision could come from your own mind, like a daydream, your mind will not cause an open vision that is seen externally and cannot be stopped. These are obviously from the Lord. Additionally, open visions may be seen by more than one person at the same time.

DREAMS

Dreams are another common way in which the Lord speaks. In the first two chapters of Matthew's Gospel, we find that Joseph, Mary's husband, received four distinct dreams from God that were instructional in nature. He was told to take Mary as his wife, to flee with his family to

Egypt, to return to Israel, and to turn aside and dwell in Galilee. There are several different types of dreams that the Lord gives (see Matthew 1:20, 2:13, 2:20, 2:22).

1) Literal Dreams

Literal dreams are simply quick vignettes, showing us the future under certain circumstances. Many times these short dreams are easier to understand because they need little or no interpretation. Often I have this type of dream after an incidental contact with a person whom I do not normally encounter.

As an example, I received a short phone call one day from a man I knew, but I had not seen in approximately two years. That night I had a dream that this man and his wife sold their home to buy a larger, more expensive one. When they did, their business began a downward spiral, and they were on their way to losing the new house when my dream ended.

The next morning I found his phone number, called him and asked if he was planning to buy a new house. When he said yes, I told him about the dream. They felt my dream was indeed from the Lord and decided not to sell their existing home. Within months, he experienced the downturn in his business that I had seen in my dream. They were able to survive financially because they had not incurred the extra expenses of a larger home.

2) Symbolic Dreams

Other dreams can be highly symbolic in nature and must be carefully interpreted over time and often with much prayer and meditation. Some symbolic dreams are highly personal ways God uses to speak to people about decisions facing them. Many people are "metaphorically oriented," and God speaks often to them in symbolic dreams.

A friend of mine was trying to make a decision concerning the education of her children. Since it involved a significant change in their current direction, she prayed over her choices for several days, but received no answer. When asked by a friend if she was going to make the change, she told them that she had not received a green light yet.

A day later, she dreamed of driving a car that was stopped at an intersection. When she looked up at the traffic light, the cars in front of her had already moved on and she had a green light. The dream ended. When she awoke, she heard the Lord say, "Go forward." She made the change, and it bore good fruit in her children.

3) Dreams of Angels or the Lord

Some dreams consist simply of an angel or the Lord speaking to us. These are not visitations; they are dreams, but they are a high level of revelation. There are a number of scriptural examples of these types of dreams (see Genesis 20:3, 31:24; I Kings 3:5-15; Matthew 1:20; 2:12-13).

God not only speaks to prophets in dreams, but He speaks to moms, carpenters, managers, executives, children—almost everyone. Many children in our fellowship regularly receive warnings, encouragements, and excellent teachings from God in dreams. God is desiring to speak to us, and dreams are one of His most effective ways.

TRANCES

Do not be afraid of this designation. Trances are found in the New Testament. Peter fell into a trance in which

God profoundly spoke to him. Through obedience to the instructions he was given in the trance, Peter received a revelation that the gospel was for the Gentiles as well as the Jews (see Acts 10:34). When he acted on this message, the door of faith was opened to the Gentiles.

During a trance, most, if not all awareness of your natural surroundings is obscured, and you are transfixed on the events in the trance as opposed to an open vision where you *observe* something transpiring. In a trance, you *participate* in a scene through your actions. They can last any length of time—from a few seconds to several hours. Church history is filled with accounts of God speaking through trances.

One prophetic friend of mine periodically falls into trances where the Lord gives him revelation on a much higher level than he normally experiences. God will often give him the names of people and what will transpire in their lives in the next twelve months. We have seen powerful revelation received through this means.

Trances are a higher level of revelation than dreams or visions, again because they are less subjective in nature. You cannot make yourself have a trance; they come from the Lord and do not stop until He stops them.

Being Caught up in the Spirit

This is similar to a trance, except you seem to be transported somewhere. Do not be disturbed by this type of revelation or even its description. This is a biblical experience.

Paul was caught up in the Spirit into the third heaven. He was not sure if this happened with his spirit leaving his body or if he was actually caught up bodily to the third heaven (see II Corinthians 12:23). Although those in the New Age and the occult have experiences that counterfeit being caught up in the Spirit, such as astral projection, we must understand that God is the Creator. Satan has never created anything and can only counterfeit.

Ezekiel also experienced being caught up in the Spirit (see Ezekiel 3:12-15). However, this did not cease with Ezekiel and Paul. God still uses experiences like these to speak to His people today.

ANGELIC VISITATIONS

It is amazing to see how often angels brought messages to the saints in the Book of Acts. They often came in dreams or visions, but come they did. We have almost lost the concept that angels are messengers. We have relegated them to a category of heavenly protectors or heavenly worshipers. While they do perform these functions, the word "angel" means "messenger."

God continues to speak in this fashion today. The appearance of angels is increasing and often occurs before a significant spiritual advance for the church. We must understand that God will speak this way to many of us. Paul had angels speak to him (see Acts 27:23-24), and Peter was released from prison by an angel who physically appeared and literally opened locked doors for him.

VISITATIONS OF THE LORD

Not only will angels appear to us, but the Lord Himself will also visit some people. Like angels, He will often come in dreams, visions, or even reveal Himself visibly to us. This is obviously the highest level of prophetic revelation possible. John, the Apostle, received the Book of Revelation from an actual visitation of Jesus. Paul also had a visitation from the Lord (see Acts 9:37).

While there are no clearly defined instructions on how to hear God in Scripture, we do find examples of God speaking through impressions, visions, dreams, trances, and angels. Throughout the Book of Acts, we find God speaking through all of these means to His people (see Acts 5:2-5; 5:19; 8:26-30; 9:10; 9:34; 10:3; 10:10-20; 12:7; 13:2; 14:9; 16:9; 18:9).

KEYS TO HEARING GOD

In order to recognize God's voice, we must pay attention. One encounter from my life dramatically illustrates this point. One of the first times I ministered with Bob Jones, a seasoned prophetic man, I received a stern correction for not paying attention to what I felt in my body.

Bob and I had been ministering for most of the day and I was worn-out. Bob, meanwhile, was going strong. I decided to take a break and went to the back of the room and sat down approximately twenty feet behind Bob as he continued ministering to a young woman. I began rubbing my right eye which had started itching. As soon as I did this, Bob, with his back still turned to me, yelled, "Steve, that's not just your eye that's itching—it's God speaking to you about *her* eye. You've got to pay attention!" Needless to say, I started paying attention.

As you minister, *pay attention!* The Lord will give you impressions for others. That is what ministry is about— serving others. Remember, we are asking for bread for others on their journey. God will give us all we need, but we must pay attention in order to receive it. Listed below are some disciplines that will help us be more sensitive to recognizing when God is giving us revelation.

1. ***Dwell in His presence***—As we cultivate the presence of the Lord in our lives, we are made more aware of when God speaks. This occurs as we spend consistent time with Him devotionally. Through worship and meditation in the Scriptures, we can begin to dwell in His presence.

2. ***Focus on God's purposes***—As we cultivate a deepening commitment to the purposes of God, we position ourselves to receive prophetic revelation from Him. Amos 3:7 says that He will do nothing except He reveal it to His servants, the prophets. Part of being prophetic is being a servant of the Lord. A servant's highest goal is to see his Master's purposes succeed.

3. ***Ask God continually***—The Lord desires to give us the kingdom (see Luke 12:32). Like any parent, He loves it when we are eager and hungry to help others. If we ask the Lord for prophetic revelation in order to minister to others, He will speak to us.

4. ***Grow in love toward others***—The spiritual gifts are given so we can effectively minister God's grace to others. True discernment is a byproduct of godly love (see Philippians 1:9). Faith works by love, and as we grow in love for others, we are positioning ourselves to receive prophetic revelation from the Lord.

5. ***Do a "body check"***—Whenever I enter a meeting or am talking with someone, I do an initial "body check." I recognize that God may give me impressions in my spirit, soul, or body. Then, as I am ministering, I am aware of my total being and am

open to God using impressions to speak to me about a person or situation.

6. *Become a lover of God's written Word*—The Bible is our more sure Word of prophecy. If we love God's Word and feed our soul on it, we will begin to grow in our sensitivity to His spoken word as well.

By making these disciplines a part of our lives, we will grow in our sensitivity to the Lord and His voice. As we grow in sensitivity to the ways He speaks, we will be amazed at how clearly we can receive revelation we at one time did not even notice. When we begin consistently recognizing His voice, we then need to begin developing our ability to interpret the prophetic revelation we receive.

Chapter Four

INTERPRETING REVELATION

The next step for growing in prophetic ministry is learning to accurately interpret the revelation we receive from God. We discovered in the last chapter that most Christians are already hearing God's voice, but many do not recognize it. Still others recognize *when* He speaks, but do not understand *what* He is saying. Until we understand the meaning of the revelation, we will not be consistently fruitful in prophetic ministry. Understanding is the essence of interpretation.

As stated previously, there are three components of a prophetic word: *revelation, interpretation,* and *application.* Interpretation is the pivotal component since it involves understanding what God is saying. Interpretation is also where most people make mistakes.

The goal of this chapter is to explain the types of symbolism God uses and to provide guidelines and principles for interpreting revelation. However, before proceeding toward this goal, we need to acknowledge certain truths that will govern and temper our discussion.

WHY THE SECRECY?

As we identified in chapter three, God speaks in unusual ways. We discussed these different ways in order to recognize His word regardless of how it comes. Now we need to briefly examine why He speaks in such unusual ways. Why doesn't God just speak clearly and plainly to us?

He does this for several reasons. One reason is outlined by a young prophetic man named Elihu in the story of Job.

Indeed God speaks once, or twice, yet no one notices it.

In a dream, a vision of the night, when sound sleep falls on men, while they slumber in their beds,

Then He opens the ears of men, and seals their instruction,

That He may turn man aside from his conduct, and keep man from pride (Job 33:14-17).

God wants to draw us closer to Him. He delights in using unusual and strange means to speak to us, drawing us away from the mundane routine of our lives to pursue Him. Since most of us are prone to living our lives independent of Him, He uses something unusual to catch our attention and draw us to Himself. He speaks in a cryptic fashion so that we have to seek Him for understanding.

Many times He will use a vision, dream, impression, or some other phenomenon to get our attention. When we are captured by the phenomenon and begin investigating, God then speaks to us and brings us into His presence.

Turn Aside to See

If we do not turn aside to investigate the phenomenon the Lord initiates, we will not hear His voice. A clear example of this is found in God's call for Moses to return to Egypt as the deliverer of Israel.

Now Moses was pasturing the flock of Jethro his father-in-law, the priest of Midian;

and he led the flock to the west side of the wilderness, and came to Horeb, the mountain of God.

And the angel of the LORD appeared to him in a blazing fire from the midst of a bush; and he looked, and behold, the bush was burning with fire, yet the bush was not consumed.

So Moses said, "I must turn aside now, and see this marvelous sight, why the bush is not burned up."

When the LORD saw that he turned aside to look, God called to him from the midst of the bush, and said, "Moses, Moses!" And he said, "Here I am" (Exodus 3:1-4).

For forty years, Moses had been following sheep around the wilderness. One day he sees a bush that is burning, but not being consumed. This sight so captures his attention that Moses leaves his daily routine and turns aside to examine this strange sight. Verse 4 says that when the Lord **"saw"** that Moses turned aside to look, *then* God spoke to him.

INTERDEPENDENCE AND DEPENDENCE

Another reason God speaks to us in unusual ways is because of His desire for us to recognize our interdependence on the body of Christ. Many times, those who receive the revelation have the least ability to interpret revelation. Many who receive interpretations have the least amount of revelatory gifting. We must fit together to see the plan of God. We will miss out on much that God has for us if we do not learn to cooperate with one another.

Another reason God speaks in unusual ways is to preserve the preciousness of His words. If God were to constantly blurt out words to us without our having to seek Him further, we would not appreciate or esteem His words properly. Anything worth having is worth searching for. When we have to seek Him for understanding, we will esteem what He reveals as precious. **"It is the glory of God to conceal a thing: but the honour of kings is to search out a matter" (Proverbs 25:2 KJV).**

Because I understand these principles and appreciate them, this chapter was difficult to write. I am wary of presenting a list of symbols and a system of interpretation that keeps anyone from depending on God. If I enable you to operate independent of a relationship with Jesus, I have done you the greatest disservice possible under the guise of prophetic equipping.

Therefore, instead of providing a comprehensive list of symbols and their meanings, I will provide some examples of how the Lord has used certain symbols and how they have been interpreted. My goal is that you see *how* God uses different symbols to speak to us. Study to see the principles of how God uses symbols and how to interpret, instead of attempting to memorize what individual symbols "always" represent.

A More Sure Word of Prophecy

We do have a more sure word of prophecy (see II Peter 1:19). The Bible is one of the most precious gifts God has given us. Men and women throughout history have been martyred in order to preserve the Scriptures, so that we might have access to them in our own language. We should regard the written Word of God with the greatest esteem and base our doctrine and foundation for life upon it, not on spoken prophecy.

Additionally, all prophetic revelation that is received must be "filtered" through the written Word of God. Any prophetic interpretation that contradicts Scripture must be judged as inaccurate. The Bible is our grounding influence and our "baseline" for prophecy. Spoken prophecy should never replace nor supercede our dependence on the written Word for instruction and doctrine.

SCRIPTURAL SYMBOLISM

The first type of symbolism God uses is *scriptural symbolism.* Because the Bible is foundational to our walk with God, He often uses symbols which find their origin in Scripture when He gives prophetic revelation. There are several reasons for this. First, we are to hold the Bible in the highest esteem and be generally familiar with its symbols. Second, by directing us to symbols found in the Bible, we are brought into contact with the written Word which has power to establish our souls.

In an illustration referred to in chapter three, as I was praying for a woman I looked at her hands and saw that they were as white as snow. I immediately thought of the Scripture from Isaiah 1:18 about the purifying work of the Lord in our lives. As I looked again, her hands had returned to a normal color. God wanted this woman to know that He saw her hands as pure as snow, not red with sin. When I told her this, she began weeping as God freed her from a recurring accusation over something for which she had been wrongly blamed in the past.

Many times, the Lord uses scriptural symbolism because there will be additional encouragement or revelation in a verse from which the symbol is referenced. When we give the Scripture that supports our revelation, there is twice as much encouragement released to the person than if we had simply given the prophetic revelation without the accompanying Scripture.

In order to interpret scriptural symbolism, we need to know God's written Word. It is important to spend as much time as possible becoming grounded in the Bible. In addition to helping us interpret revelation, it is amazing how our lives will change as we begin hiding God's Word in our hearts.

"CHAPTER AND VERSE" SCRIPTURES

Many times God will speak "chapter and verse" Scriptures to us. We will hear a reference for a specific chapter and verse and not know how the verse reads. When we examine the passage, we will find that there is a powerful message for us in the verse, either in its actual meaning, according to the context of Scripture, or in a "pietistic way." This method of interpretation entails the verse being taken out of context and the words applying specifically and literally to a given situation.

Several years ago, a wonderful Christian family moved to Charlotte to join our new church plant, but were not yet involved in any ministry. They had not obtained jobs at this point, but were in good shape financially. In fact, they did not need to work in order to support themselves.

During this time of transition, the couple became somewhat passive in their souls. Without any real intention of doing so, they stopped moving forward in faith and geared their energy toward wondering. While waiting for a prophetic word to direct them, they wondered: *What are we supposed to do?* They soon became mired in inactivity and began tottering in their faith while waiting to hear what they were to do.

As I prayed for this couple, I simply asked, "Lord, what *are* they supposed to do?" Immediately, I heard the Lord speak into my spirit, "Acts 22:10." Not knowing how this verse read, I looked it up and found the following:

> **And I said, What shall I do, Lord? And the Lord said unto me, Arise, and go into Damascus; and there it shall be told thee of all things which are appointed for thee to do (KJV).**

This chapter and verse reference included my friends' question and their answer. I just did not understand the answer. I knew the Lord was not suggesting that they go to the city of Damascus to receive guidance, so I searched for the meaning of Damascus. When I looked up the word "Damascus," I found that it means "activity or action." The Lord was saying to this couple, *Arise, and go into action or activity, and there in the place of being active it shall be told you of all things which are appointed for you to do.*

Every word in Scripture has meaning, including proper names. For this reason, I carry a *Scripture Proper Names Dictionary* in order to be prepared when the Lord gives me a proper name in a prophetic situation. There are many other ways the Lord will speak to us through "chapter and verse" Scriptures.

Early in my Christian walk, the Lord told me that if I did not get up at 4:00 a.m., I would miss hearing what He had to say to me for that day. I was not too thrilled at the prospect of getting out of bed every morning at 4:00 a.m., so I asked the Lord to confirm this word. Fifteen minutes later, the Lord spoke the following chapter and verse reference to me: *Ezekiel 12:8.* I looked it up and found that the verse said, **"And in the morning came the word of the Lord unto me..."** (Ezekiel 12:8 KJV).

This was a powerful confirmation of an unusual word, but I could not deny it no matter how hard I tried. As a caution, this is not simply "playing" Bible roulette. We are not spinning the wheel of the Bible and seeing where it lands. If you believe that you heard a chapter and verse reference and find it does not exist, then you can judge that word as inaccurate. If you receive a Scripture that makes no sense, go ahead and research it, but realize that sometimes we are hearing our own human spirit, not the Lord's.

CONTEMPORARY SYMBOLISM

Contemporary symbolism does not originate from the Bible, but is drawn from contemporary life. These symbols speak to us through what they represent in our daily lives or in our societal norms. Just as Jesus spoke consistently in parables drawn from the contemporary life of Israel, God will speak to us in parables using contemporary symbols as well.

For example, the Lord will often use motorcycles, automobiles, buses, trucks, and airplanes to speak of ministries. These symbols are not found in the Bible because they did not exist then, but they still hold meaning for us. Let's consider what these items have in common and also how they are different.

Each of these objects is a vehicle of transportation. One thing God shows me fairly consistently is the spiritual gifts and ministries to which people are called. God often uses these symbols to speak of the different *vehicles of ministry* in which He has called people to function. Whereas, a car may speak of local ministry or personal ministry, a bus may speak of a congregation or ministry organization because it is often used to transport teams of people. Airplanes can speak of national or international ministry because their range of travel is greater than others.

Motorcycles have been used to speak of prophetic ministry for a number of reasons. When riding a motorcycle, you have increased vision, quicker acceleration, greater maneuverability, extreme stability at high speeds, and less protection. Also a motorcycle rider is sensitive to changes in the elements when he rides. All of these are indicative of those ministering prophetically.

EXAMPLE #1

During a conference, a woman who was working on our prophetic teams was ministering to a couple in their fifties when she saw a vision of an airplane taking off. She told them their best years were yet to come and they were called to minister in evangelism internationally. Tears came to their eyes as they began to relate their story to her. The husband had been an airline pilot for TWA for over twenty years and was retiring in one month to begin ministering full-time in evangelism.

In this case, God used a symbol that our team member understood, but also one holding special meaning for this couple. Because the symbol of the airplane was so personal to them and spoke prophetically of their calling, it brought extra confirmation to them, which they needed. The airplane spoke of a national or international ministry; that it was taking off represented that this couple was just getting ready to begin (or take off) in ministry.

Example #2

Another powerful example of God using contemporary symbolism involves a dream my brother, Eddie, received some years ago. In his dream, my brother arrived at a place of business for a job interview, but did not know what job he was applying for. A man appeared and said to him, "We've been waiting for you." He then seated my brother in a large room that was being used for a restaurant in which there were many people eating.

My brother asked the man what he was supposed to be doing. The gentleman said, "You are supposed to feed these people." My brother began to protest, saying he had never fed such a large number of people before and did not know how to do this. Eddie then saw our father seated in the restaurant, who had prepared food for large crowds at church functions for years. Eddie told the man that he could not feed these people, but that our father could. The man smiled and said, "Yes, he will help you."

My brother then asked the man how many people he would be responsible to feed. The man replied, "181 at first, but later you will be responsible for feeding 500." Suddenly, a gentleman stood up and began singing a country song accompanied by a guitar. My brother turned to someone sitting next to him and said, "I hate country music." The country song ended fairly quickly and the dream ended.

When he received this dream, my brother was a successful businessman, but knew he was called to ministry. Several weeks prior, he had been asked to pastor a small rural congregation in a neighboring town. Having never pastored before and having little ministry experience, he felt unqualified and was reluctant to accept the position.

When he awoke from the dream, he realized God was calling him to pastor this congregation. When he agreed to do so, he was shocked to learn that there were exactly 181 active members, which matched the number of people he was responsible to feed in the dream.

Consider the symbolism God used in this dream and how it spoke perfectly into his situation. Eddie was offered a job feeding people. This is biblical symbolism because the word pastor means "a feeder." However, restaurants are not biblical symbols, but contemporary symbols.

In the dream, Eddie saw our father sitting at the restaurant. He knew that our father could do this job, but Eddie was unsure of himself. The man in the dream told Eddie that our father would help him. This did not mean that our natural father would be involved in this congregation with Eddie; it meant that our heavenly Father would help Eddie do His will. Our natural father represented God (our Father) in this dream.

The symbols in the dream continued. My brother really does hate country music, and this symbol represented that God understood his not wanting to go to a rural or country church. My brother's likes and dislikes did not change God's will, but God was acknowledging what was in Eddie's heart.

After accepting the position, God blessed this rural church and they experienced new life and new growth. In the dream, the country music only lasted a short time. This was also a symbol. Eddie only pastored this congregation for about sixteen months before leaving to pastor a new church plant in a metropolitan area. That congregation has grown from fifty to four hundred people in the eight years he has been serving as their pastor.

He continues to draw insight and understanding from this dream. He knows that his current commission eventually entails responsibility for feeding five hundred people because this was the word given in his dream.

Interpreting Impressions

God often speaks to many people through impressions in their bodies. We identified this in the last chapter. The Lord trained me in my early days of ministry to recognize different physical impressions as representing different emotional or spiritual conflicts. Some of these impressions had a scriptural basis for their interpretation; others had a contemporary basis for interpretation.

Many times I feel a burning, painful sensation in my left shoulder blade when praying for someone. When I first received this impression, I was unsure what it meant. Later, the Lord showed me that these people had been wounded by a serious betrayal from someone with whom they were close. I realized that this physical sensation was identical to the pain someone would feel if they were literally "stabbed in the back." Being stabbed in the back is a figure of speech representing betrayal. This is the basis for the interpretation.

Other times, I receive an impression in the area of my body where my gall bladder is located. When I first received this impression, I realized that in Scripture gall speaks of bitterness (see Jeremiah 9:15, Acts 8:23). In each case, the people to whom I was ministering were dealing with a situation that was causing or could cause them to become bitter. Rather than accusing them of bitterness, I addressed the situation and offered to walk them through the process of forgiveness.

PERSONAL SYMBOLISM

Another type of symbolism God uses to speak is *personal symbolism*. These symbols are common to our culture, but also hold special meaning for individuals because of personal experience. There are many places, events, and things that hold great significance for me due to my life experiences, but which may be relatively meaningless to others.

I was praying for a couple once who had never heard of prophetic ministry, and this was their first time attending our congregation. As I prayed, I saw a quick internal vision of a golf club. Because I play golf, I knew by certain details in the vision that it was a one wood, which is called a "driver." I also received certain other details about this couple as I prayed for them.

As I pondered the meaning of the golf club vision, I realized God was showing me that one of them was a "driver" as a profession. When I asked them if this was true, they were both shocked, as the man drove a bulldozer for a living. This simple piece of revelation opened their hearts to receive the other things the Lord wanted to speak to them.

At other times when praying for people, I have seen a vision of a dog standing next to them. When dogs are mentioned in Scripture, it is almost always negative in nature. But I love dogs based on my personal experience and they bring to my mind friendship, faithfulness, and loyalty. Every time I have seen a dog, the encouragement for the person was that God had positioned someone next to them who would be a faithful, loyal, and true friend to them.

However, if I receive a vision of a menacing-looking dog that was postured aggressively toward someone, I would not prophesy to them about loyalty and faithfulness. Instead, I would offer them a warning.

A Long and Winding Road

Sometimes, the pathway to an interpretation is long and winding. As I prayed for a young man at the end of a very long meeting, I could feel a very gentle sensation on my teeth. It felt as if one of my teeth was being removed. Some years previously, the Lord had used teeth as a symbol to speak to me about relationships. As I pondered this, I felt like God was showing me that a relationship had been removed from this man's life and that he had many questions about it. I began ministering to him based on this revelation and interpretation.

I told him, "God has removed a relationship from your life. It was God's will for this relationship to end. You have many questions about it, but this was from the Lord." When I said this, his face turned red, and he began breathing rapidly as God's power came upon him.

While this was happening, the Lord showed me by discernment three specific assignments from the enemy against his life that could keep him from fulfilling his ministry. I then prayed for him, breaking these things off of his life. His countenance changed before my eyes.

As I talked with him later, I was amazed at his story. He had been dating and was interested in marrying a wonderful Christian girl. However, they were led to end their relationship, believing that God had shown them to do so. Afterward, he was left with many questions. This was the relationship that the Lord had shown me was removed from his life. However, there was more.

When he was only three months old, his father had died tragically. At that point, the enemy assigned rejection, fear of abandonment, and depression against him. As he grew older, the enemy gained some access to his life through the wounds in his soul surrounding his father's tragic death. When he ended his engagement years later, all three of these issues—rejection, fear of abandonment, and depression—began plaguing him again.

When I prophesied concerning the removal of this relationship, these three issues were uncovered, and we were able to break their assignment against his life. He immediately experienced a level of victory he had not previously known in his Christian walk. He works today as the youth pastor of a thriving congregation.

I walked away from this encounter with a greater fear of the Lord than I can describe. A young man was delivered into the plan of God for his life because God gave me an impression that I felt in my teeth! There was a need for sensitivity to recognize the revelation, then a need for a certain level of scriptural knowledge and understanding of God's purposes to interpret and apply the revelation. It all fit together to provide healing and deliverance for this young man.

SYMBOLS OR CYMBALS

Some of you are wondering why teeth symbolized relationships in the previous example. In Song of Solomon 4:2 and 6:6, the bride's teeth are described as flocks of sheep. **"Your teeth are like a flock of shorn sheep..." (see Song of Solomon 4:2 NKJV).** Sheep in Scripture generally represent people, and flocks speak of groups of people or relationships.

While this may be a complicated way for God to simply say "relationships," it is an effective one. The Lord began using the symbol of teeth to speak to my wife and me almost ten years ago. Whenever God uses symbols with such a personal meaning, it is not a subtle message—it is very loud. This is when a symbol becomes a "cymbal," which is a loud exclamation to finalize a point.

What Meaneth This?

While there are some general guidelines about interpretation, there are no established patterns or formulas. God will not use the same symbol to speak the same message to everyone, but there are some symbols which seem to be common to many prophetic ministers.

When I began ministering with Bob Jones, I discovered that God had been speaking to us with the same symbolism. God had taught both of us that certain impressions in particular places on our body represented the same thing. Most had a scriptural basis for what they represented. Examples of this included how we both discerned depression, attacks on someone's faith, and a religious spirit. The impressions that did not have a scriptural precedent for their interpretation had a contemporary basis for the interpretation.

On many occasions, as I have ministered to individuals or couples whom I did not know, the first thing I would see as I prayed was the roof of a house. The Lord impressed upon me that this represented that they were *covered* and I would prophesy this to them. "Covering" throughout Scripture speaks of protection and safety.

In every case to date, these people had at one time been part of a group which overemphasized being in proper relationship with the church or church leadership. They had been told by the leadership of these congregations that their lives would fall apart if they ever left their particular group. In these cases, the Lord used the prophetic symbol of a roof to break curses off of them and to release them into the freedom and truth of God.

Consider the symbol of a bed. Many times, we have seen a bed perfectly prepared with a storm swirling around it, or in other cases a bed that is disheveled. These symbols are relatively easy to interpret. The bed that is perfectly prepared with a storm surrounding it could represent the Lord giving this person rest (a bed is a place of rest) in the midst of a stormy and difficult time. A bed that is disheveled can represent that the enemy is attempting to disturb the person's ability to rest in the Lord or to be at peace.

Understanding the meaning of symbols and concepts in Scripture is imperative to interpreting prophetic revelation. But having an index of symbols and their meanings is less important than having an overall understanding and knowledge of Scripture at large. **"But the Helper, the Holy Spirit, whom the Father will send in My name, He will teach you all things, and bring to your remembrance all that I said to you" (John 14:26).**

The Holy Spirit is the One helping us with interpretations, and He will remind us of examples from Scripture. Knowing God's Word, and understanding it, is foundational to accurately interpreting prophetic revelation.

DETAILS AND DISTINCTIONS ARE IMPORTANT

When we receive a vision, dream, or impression, each detail is often significant. If we see a hand in a vision, was it a right hand or a left hand? If we have an impression, what does the impression "feel like?" The distinctions we make can often make the difference in our interpretation. Accurate interpretation is our goal, and details often provide the greatest clues.

The word "discern" means to "distinguish between." The ability to distinguish between details is often very important when seeking an interpretation. While a vision of a right hand may carry one very specific message, a vision of a left hand may mean something entirely different. This is addressed in several examples in the next chapter.

The Pun Is Mightier Than the Sword

As we mentioned in chapter three, God will use a "play on words" to speak to us as He did in Jeremiah 1:11-12. Again, this is not us wrangling an interpretation—this is God using a word picture to emphasize a point.

Several years ago, I began meeting with the local pastors in our city. About a year after becoming involved, God began moving. A number of congregations came together to sponsor joint meetings and God showed up in power. Immediately afterward, the pastor who had really led this effort was betrayed by another pastor who wanted to lead instead. The other pastors had stood by passively while this occurred. I had not witnessed this transpiring, but had received a prophetic revelation about this situation.

I knew I was to address this situation, but I was uncomfortable because I was at least ten years younger than these pastors whom I respected. When I confronted them with the prophetic revelation and warning God had given me, the majority of the pastors denounced me and the prophetic word I gave.

As I left the pastors meeting, the enemy began accusing me of being divisive, unsubmissive, and critical. I began thinking I should have remained quiet and supported the joint meetings they were planning. The enemy was having a heyday with my mind.

Later that evening while I was teaching a prophetic class, someone received a vision for me. They were praying for me and saw a picture of a wagon wheel. I knew this vision was from the Lord, but had no interpretation. We all began praying for an interpretation and waited on the Lord. Suddenly one lady exclaimed, "You're outspoken," and the presence of God filled the room.

A wagon wheel is comprised of a series of spokes that stretch out from a center hub. God was saying that I was made by Him to be like a wagon wheel—"out-spoke-en." Without the students knowing what I was going through, God silenced the accusations and answered my own questions. Within a week, the warning which I had spoken to the pastors came to pass also. This was the last real struggle I had concerning my calling to be outspoken. God had spoken loudly and clearly—now, so do I.

DON'T FORGET THE BIG PICTURE

Although details are often important, they may sometimes obscure what God is trying to say. Sometimes the details are not as important as the general message or the bigger picture. When you become comfortable in your "detail-the-distinctions" strategy, God will change His method. Then the details of a revelation will be insignificant, relative to the interpretation. Often, this is the way God speaks in dreams.

One of our pastor's wives had a dream that troubled her. She was riding in the backseat of a minivan being driven by her eight-year-old daughter. Her daughter is a prophetic child and has often represented the emerging prophetic ministry in dreams and visions that a number of us have received.

They happened upon an accident, and the daughter spun the van out of control by overreacting to it. Her mother ran forward from the rear of the van to gain control of the vehicle in time to keep it from crashing, and the van came to rest gently in a ditch. While coming forward from the rear seat, this pastor's wife was gripped with the fear of losing her license for allowing her daughter to drive. Then the dream ended.

One of our prophetic councils was trying to interpret this dream. They immediately began breaking the dream into different parts and applying interpretative principles, trying to decode each symbol in the dream to get the overall message. I sensed confusion enter the room, so I stopped the process and suggested we pray instead. As we waited on the Lord, one person received this word: "What is apparent?" The Lord was showing us the key to interpreting this dream.

Instead of trying to piece together all the different symbolism, we looked at what was apparent in the dream. This was apparent: An eight-year-old should not be driving the vehicle, regardless of how gifted she is. Since this young girl often represented the emerging or young prophetic ministry, we understood that God was giving us this message: "Don't let the emerging prophetic ministry drive the ministry." Instead of wrangling through endless symbolic possibilities, we saw the simple, but profound, truth.

There were other detailed portions of this dream which I have not bothered to list because they were unimportant in this case. Although this was a deeply detailed dream, the Lord was trying to speak one specific message: The prophetic is called to navigate, not to *drive* the ministry.

We must not miss the forest (overall message) for the trees (the details). Although details are important, they are not the message; they only point to it. Do not get bogged down in the details.

THE IMPORTANCE OF CONTEXT

There are other factors to be considered in interpreting dreams and visions. If the revelation is to be properly interpreted, we must ensure that the details are not taken out of context in our interpretation when the whole dream is not from the Lord (many times only a brief portion of a dream is from God).

A friend stopped by my office one day with a dream he had received. In his dream, he was playing soccer. He assisted on two goals and scored another one. He got so excited that during one point in the dream, he tried to "punch" the ball into the goal using his hand, which is illegal in soccer, but this did not result in a goal. Then his dream ended.

My friend understood this dream to be speaking about evangelism. The Lord was instructing him to either get people born again or to assist those who are doing it. This was what scoring or assisting on the goals represented (the previous week he had led one person to Christ and helped as someone else led two others to salvation). He then said, "The Lord said to do whatever we have to, even cheating if we have to, but get people born again!" This last point was his interpretation of his attempt to "punch" the ball into the goal with his hand.

I agreed with every point in his interpretation except the last one. When I mentioned that he did not score when he cheated, it stunned him. Being a humble man, he admitted that within the context of the dream, this interpretation did not fit. In fact, we then reinterpreted this as a revelation of why many of the "salvations" in the church have not accomplished the goal. Man's hand was involved, and this is illegal.

Just as Scripture taken out of context often can be easily misinterpreted and misapplied, the same happens with some prophetic interpretations as well. Since context is a part of the bigger picture, we must keep this in mind when interpreting revelation. But do not make "keeping things in context" your new system of interpretation. Keep depending on God.

God Is Not "Mr. Spock"

God does not always speak in symbols that are logically interpreted. One obstacle to understanding what God is saying is that some interpretations cannot be rationally or logically derived. Sometimes an interpretation must be received just like revelation.

Many interpretations in Daniel and Joseph's lives could not be logically deduced, even in hindsight. It is important to remember that interpretation, like revelation, often will be received from God without any work on our part, other than seeking Him.

In this same vein, there are people who have a gift of interpretation, but cannot explain how they receive their interpretations. If they try to explain it, we will often lose confidence in the interpretation. Some who are less linear in their thinking are often much better at interpretation than those who think rationally and logically.

INTERPRETATIONS ARE NOT OPINIONS

Interpretations are not opinions. Interpretation is much more than offering our idea of what a revelation means. It is imperative to learn to discern the anointing or "witness" of God upon an interpretation. God often leads us by His presence, and He will lead us to an interpretation in this way as well. Many times, when someone begins getting "off course" in their quest to interpret, I will feel a confusion in my soul. This is God's way of letting us know we are looking in the wrong place.

BALANCE AND WISDOM

We have no formulas, patterns, or templates of prophetic interpretation. As we gain knowledge of certain symbols, we must gain wisdom and understanding as well. Whenever we begin to develop a system of symbolism, we must be aware that when God speaks symbolically, He can use the same symbols to represent many different things.

What does the symbol of a serpent represent? Evil, Satan, or deception? These could all be valid interpretations, since each has a scriptural precedent. However, a serpent can also represent Jesus or healing. The brazen serpent raised on a pole in the wilderness was a type and shadow of Jesus being lifted up (see John 3:14-15). The serpent entwined on a staff is also a contemporary symbol of the medical profession which can speak prophetically of healing.

Here is the warning: If there is a symbol that can represent either Satan or Jesus, we'd better be listening to God and not just depending on a system of interpretation.

In addition, we are not relegated to dependence on the ideas of men. We have something better than a system of interpretation—we serve a living God who speaks living words to us.

False Prophecy or Misinterpretation?

In many cases, much of what would be considered false prophecy is accurate, but misinterpreted, revelation. Someone may receive a clear picture from God, but then misinterpret or misapply it. This does not make their revelation false; it just needs to be interpreted accurately.

In Acts 21, we find an interesting case of a true prophetic revelation being misinterpreted to some degree and also misapplied by some as well.

> **And as we tarried there many days, there came down from Judaea a certain prophet, named Agabus.**
>
> **And when he was come unto us, he took Paul's girdle, and bound his own hands and feet, and said, Thus saith the Holy Ghost, So shall the Jews at Jerusalem bind the man that owneth this girdle, and shall deliver him into the hands of the Gentiles.**
>
> **And when we heard these things, both we, and they of that place, besought him not to go up to Jerusalem (Acts 21:10-12 KJV).**

Agabus prophesied that the Jews at Jerusalem would bind Paul, hand and foot, and deliver him to the Gentiles. However, what actually happened was that the Jews took Paul and were about to kill him when the Gentiles came and delivered him from the Jews. Then the Gentiles bound him, not the Jews.

Even though Agabus got some of the details confused, this was still a profound prophetic revelation. I do not believe that Paul walked around in jail, complaining about Agabus and his false prophecy. It was an accurate revelation, with minor details confused in the interpretation.

There was also a problem with the application for some people. In verse 12, many who heard the prophetic word thought that this was a directive for Paul to avoid going to Jerusalem. In actuality, it was just the Lord preparing Paul for what he would face in Jerusalem. He had been shown years earlier that he would suffer for the Lord (see Acts 9:16).

AVOIDING MISINTERPRETATIONS

In other instances, God will show us symbols that seemingly have little significance at all. However, as we report what we see without interpretation, the results are often amazing. This is also one way to minimize the possibility of misinterpreting revelation. We simply report what we have seen without muddying the water with an interpretation we are unsure of.

I was ministering to a woman who was approximately sixty years old when I received an internal vision of a set of parallel bars like those used in gymnastics. I received several other revelations as well, but was confused about the parallel bars. I had difficulty connecting a sixty-year-old lady and gymnastics. Finally, after ministering the rest of the revelation to her and seeing the accuracy of what God had shown me, I told her about the vision of the parallel bars without offering any interpretation.

She began laughing and told me that she was a physical therapist who works with patients in rehabilitation. One of the things she does almost daily is work with them on parallel bars helping them to learn to walk. In this case, my inability to interpret was not harmful because I did not misinterpret: I simply gave the revelation without offering any interpretation.

While we need to pursue and grow in our ability to interpret, we must remember that God will use us right now. He will bless people through us while we are growing, but we must not use the mercy of God as an excuse to remain in the immature place we currently occupy. We need greater understanding of interpretation and greater sensitivity to the Holy Spirit to become more profitable to the Lord in ministry. In fact, my next book on the prophetic ministry will be dedicated almost exclusively to explaining and clarifying interpretation.

HINDRANCES TO ACCURATE INTERPRETATION

In addition to a lack of experience or understanding about symbolism, there are many other factors that can hinder our ability to accurately interpret the revelation we receive from God. These "heart hindrances" are the subject of our next chapter.

Chapter Five

PREPARATION FOR INTERPRETATION

In addition to understanding interpretative principles, we must also have "clean hearts" to accurately interpret prophetic revelation. Interpretations are often derived through an interplay between our understanding of interpretative principles, our sensitivity to the Holy Spirit, and our heart attitude. To accurately interpret God's mind, we must also possess His heart.

There are two basic "heart problems" that can cause misinterpretations even when we understand prophetic symbolism. The first is when our hearts are not right with God. Heart issues such as pride and "unteachableness" often cause wrong interpretations. The second problem is when our hearts are not right toward the people to whom we are ministering. These heart problems come in the form of offenses, bitterness, or prejudices. We must have our heart right toward God *and* people in order to accurately interpret prophetic revelation.

SEEING THE SIGNS, BUT MISSING THE BOAT

While praying one morning during the summer of 1995, I received a vivid vision of a polar bear. My immediate interpretation was that "a bear market in the U.S. stock exchange was coming the next winter." Later that day, I talked with Bob Jones and shared my vision with him. He immediately interpreted it as a warning of severe weather systems during the upcoming winter. Not seeing the logic of Bob's interpretation, I disagreed and published my vision and interpretation in a newsletter.

There was no "bear market" that winter, but the majority of the United States experienced the worst winter storm systems in almost one hundred years. Although I had received an accurate revelation from the Lord, I nullified any benefit it could have provided through my wrong interpretation. How could I have misinterpreted this vision so badly?

In the eighteen months previous to receiving this vision, I had begun investing in the stock market and had found myself devoting increasing amounts of my time to it. Pretty soon, I was thinking about the stock market almost constantly. When this vision came, I quickly interpreted it in light of what had become so important to me. Being so focused on the stock market, I unconsciously believed that God was focused on it as well. What appeared to me as a logical interpretation was not from God but was instead my own opinion. I was also prideful, rejecting the interpretation from a seasoned prophetic man, and instead choosing my own path.

Preparation for Interpretation

While uninterpreted revelation is often useless, misinterpreted revelation is even more disconcerting. When misinterpreted, prophetic revelation will become a stumbling stone instead of a building block. As such, we must grow in our understanding of symbolism *and* have our hearts purified as we grow closer to the Lord.

Knowing God is the single most important element in interpreting dreams, visions, and revelation—not just knowing about God or about prophetic symbolism, but knowing

Him personally. The **"testimony of Jesus is the spirit of prophecy" (see Revelation 19:10)**, so knowing Him is a key to knowing His testimony. In other words, knowing God is foundational to knowing what He is saying to us.

SCRIPTURAL EXAMPLES

Joseph and Daniel were used by God to interpret dreams and visions more than anyone else in Scripture. Although vastly different in their personalities, both knew that the foundational stone to interpretation was knowing God. While unjustly imprisoned, Joseph encountered men who were troubled by their dreams and makes this statement:

> **And they said unto him, We have dreamed a dream, and there is no interpreter of it. And Joseph said unto them, *Do not interpretations belong to God?* tell me them, I pray you (Genesis 40:8 KJV).**

Joseph's attitude at this point in his life was in stark contrast to his earlier arrogance with his family (see Genesis 37). Years of servitude and imprisonment had wrought a depth of humility in his life. His humility went even deeper after two more years of unrighteous imprisonment waiting to be remembered by Pharaoh. When Pharaoh finally called for Joseph to interpret his own dream, we find this exchange between them:

> **And Pharaoh said unto Joseph, I have dreamed a dream, and there is none that can interpret it: and I have heard say of thee, that thou canst understand a dream to interpret it.**

> **And Joseph answered Pharaoh, saying, *It is not in me: God shall give Pharaoh an answer of peace* (Genesis 41:15-16 KJV).**

Joseph knew that he was unable to interpret Pharaoh's dream. Just as Jesus could perform miracles because He knew that it was not in Himself to do it (see John 5:19), Joseph could interpret because he knew he could not. This humility positioned him to receive the interpretation from God.

Daniel also possessed this same humility. However, he was not prepared through the years of servitude, trials, and persecution that Joseph experienced. Daniel appears to have been one of those unique individuals who was able to choose humility rather than learn it through difficulty. He demonstrates this when told that the king of Babylon was troubled over a dream he had received.

> **Then Daniel went in, and desired of the king that he would give him time, and that he would show the king the interpretation.**
>
> **Then Daniel went to his house, and made the thing known to Hananiah, Mishael, and Azariah, his companions:**
>
> ***That they would desire mercies of the God of heaven concerning this secret;* that Daniel and his fellows should not perish with the rest of the wise men of Babylon.**
>
> ***Then was the secret revealed unto Daniel in a night vision. Then Daniel blessed the God of heaven*** **(Daniel 2:16-19 KJV).**

When Daniel sought God, God revealed the secret. Seeking God is humility and humility is the opposite of pride. Pride entails living life independent of God, while humility is recognizing our dependence and drawing close to Him (see James 4:6-8). The most important element of our foundation for interpretation is humility, or dependence on God.

THE PURE IN HEART SHALL SEE

In addition to humility toward God, we must also possess pure hearts toward people in order to accurately interpret prophetic revelation. Jesus said the pure in heart would see God (see Matthew 5:8), which includes accurately seeing His will. If our hearts are not pure, we will be hindered in seeing His purposes prophetically.

We must allow the Lord to root out the encumbrances which can taint our hearts. We all have some of these problems residing in our hearts, but we must strive according to His working to overcome them. If we will allow the Lord to correct us, He will continually purify us as we seek Him. Listed below are four different heart hindrances that, in addition to pride, will hinder our ability to accurately interpret revelation.

1) OPINIONS

This is a form of pride. An opinion is defined by *Webster's Dictionary* as "a judgment formed in the mind about a matter." To accurately interpret prophetic revelation, we do not need our own opinions; we need the mind of the Lord. My misinterpretation of the polar bear vision was rooted in my opinion of what was coming in the economy. Because the stock market had become so important to me, I was sure it was important to the Lord as well. Instead of seeking the Lord for an interpretation, I "logically decoded" this vision in light of my own thinking (opinions) and badly misinterpreted it.

One type of opinion, which is especially troublesome is a "pet doctrine." Pet doctrines are a danger because they are religiously motivated. A pet doctrine is a teaching that we elevate to a position of undue importance. Because it occupies an idolatrous position in our minds, our interpretations may be tainted through this idol (this is dealt with in greater detail in chapter ten). When we overemphasize any teaching, we stand in danger of interpreting prophetic revelation through the filter of that teaching.

2) Offenses and Bitterness

When we are wounded or offended by others and do not forgive them, an offense can become established in our hearts. It is all too easy to misinterpret revelation through offenses. An offense functions as "a fence" that obstructs our view of what God is saying.

You should consider suspect any negative revelation or interpretation you receive about someone who has offended you. This also includes people groups, not just individuals. Many are prone to receive accusations against members of the opposite sex due to unresolved offenses or wounds from the past. Others are prone to interpret prophetic revelation negatively and harshly toward leaders because of offenses toward past leadership. Regardless of who the offense is toward, we must be freed from them in order to accurately interpret revelation.

Forgiveness is fundamental to our walk with God and others. If we forego forgiving those who have offended us, we will soon be misinterpreting God's revelation. Instead of building, encouraging, and comforting, our revelation will be destructive and discouraging. Offenses and bitterness can have no place in our hearts if we want to be used in interpretation. Joseph's process of learning forgiveness toward unrighteous treatment is a key for us as well.

3) SIN AND SPIRITUAL BONDAGES

Another area that can hinder accurate interpretation is sin or spiritual bondage. Generally speaking, someone with a stronghold in a certain area of his or her life will suffer from poor discernment in that area.

Strongholds such as lust, bitterness, rebellion, or a religious spirit will pervert our discernment and cause us to offer inaccurate interpretations. We must be free from sin and spiritual bondages in order to accurately interpret prophetic revelation. Again, if our hearts are not pure, we will not see purely.

4) CARNAL JUDGMENT

This is related to opinion, but is more insidious because it masquerades as discernment. This is basically judging by the outward appearance. Even Samuel, arguably one of the greatest Old Testament prophets, was deceived by considering the outward appearance. Although God spoke by revelation and instructed Samuel to anoint Saul as king, Samuel took Saul's outward appearance as a testament to the Lord's grace upon him.

> **And Samuel said to all the people, *"Do you see him whom the LORD has chosen? Surely there is no one like him among all the people."* So all the people shouted and said, "Long live the king!" (I Samuel 10:24)**

Seeing is not believing in the kingdom of God. If we are judging by appearances, we will miss God. So strong is this tendency that Samuel did not learn from this first episode with Saul. When he came to anoint one of Jesse's sons as king and saw Jesse's oldest son, he makes this statement:

> **Then it came about when they entered, that he looked at Eliab and thought, "Surely the LORD's anointed is before Him."**
>
> **But the LORD said to Samuel, "Do not look at his appearance or at the height of his stature, because I have rejected him; for God sees not as man sees, for man looks at the outward appearance, but the LORD looks at the heart" (I Samuel 16:6-7).**

It is very difficult to see what God sees if we are dependent on outward appearance. We need to acknowledge this as a serious temptation in our quest to accurately interpret God's will. God's will is seldom discerned by logic or by what appears right at first glance.

In our congregation, we often minister prophetically to individuals. When we began doing this, we would have an individual or couple stand before the rest of the group so people could see them and minister prophetically to them. We still function this way in larger groups, but we have found a way that removes some of the carnal judgments from this type of ministry.

We discovered that if the group closed their eyes and did not know or see those whom they were praying for, the ministry was purer both in revelation and interpretation. When people could not see who they were praying for, they did not form instant opinions that clouded their hearts and minds. This powerfully revealed how quickly we form carnal judgments.

THE BOTTOM LINE

An ability to interpret prophetically is not developed overnight. There is a growth and maturation process which takes time. While it is possible to pass yourself off as a prophetic expert by possessing a little knowledge of symbols and some possible meanings, we must know *God*, not just principles. While we need to become more proficient in all things prophetic, we must grow in the essence of being prophetic, which is dependence on God.

Study symbolism and spend time with those who can disciple you in interpreting revelation and growing in the Lord, cultivating His presence, and learning to depend on Him. Understanding prophetic symbolism is imperative, but it is not a substitute for knowing Him. Likewise, many know Him, but are ignorant of the principles of interpretation. We cannot function at the level of prophetic insight we need to accomplish our mandate unless we have both operating in our lives.

Chapter Six

LAUNCHING INTO THE PROPHETIC
(NO ROOM FOR ERROR?)

For all ministries except one, we allow opportunities for people to grow in their gifts and abilities. No one expects teachers to be flawless, or even completely comfortable, when they first begin teaching. Nor do we require perfection of pastors when they begin their ministries. But because of misunderstandings surrounding the prophetic ministry, most of the church expects perfection from beginners. In so doing, we have effectively stopped many who were called to walk in the prophetic.

We must grow in our understanding of God. Like the children of Israel, we have seen His acts. However, we must become like Moses and understand God's *ways* (see Psalm 103:7). To have a mature prophetic ministry functioning in our congregations and in the church at large, we must first embrace immature prophetic people. As we provide a safe place for them to "try their wings," they can have a place to grow and mature.

IS GOD A HARSH JUDGE?

While preparing for a prophetic training conference where I was scheduled to minister, God dramatically confirmed my choice of messages. The Lord had instructed me to share a message entitled "No Room for Error," which I had taught once before at a conference. I do not like to speak the same message twice, so I was questioning this leading. The central theme addressed the wrong concept that unless we are 100 percent accurate in our prophecies, we must be false prophets.

At the previous conference where I shared this message, God had given me an emphatic confirmation. The day I was scheduled to speak, our local newspaper carried the headline "No Room for Error" on the front page. It was a story about the leader of the Blue Angels resigning his commission because the pressure to be perfect was destroying him. This article was a prophetic outline of my message.

The day before the current conference began, I was wrestling with sharing this same teaching. That morning, I saw the following headline in the sports section of our local newspaper: "No Room for Error." I was stunned. This was the second time that God had used the local paper to confirm my message.

This newspaper article described the absurd strictness of the judges presiding over the women's Olympic gymnastics competition. These judges penalized the young gymnasts severely for the smallest infraction. The article said that one gymnast "had made several mistakes early and had taken herself out of the competition." My message for the conference was that many had "taken themselves out of ministry because of a few small mistakes, believing that God was a harsh judge."

The first night of the conference, one of the other speakers approached me just before I was to share this message and said, "God just told me to come over here and tell you that He is not like those Olympic judges for the women's gymnastics. He is not critical and harsh with His people like that."

Why would God give so many powerful confirmations of my message? Because we desperately need to hear it. If we do not understand that God is a Father and not a harsh judge of His people, we will never have the faith necessary to begin in prophetic ministry.

MISTAKES WILL HAPPEN

When people first begin functioning in prophecy, they will make mistakes. It happens to almost everyone. Those who know God's grace and mercy are able to endure the embarrassment, failure, and sense of shame and press ahead in their callings. Others, believing that God is a harsh judge, make a few mistakes and "take themselves out of the game," thinking they have been disqualified.

God is not critical and harsh with us as we are learning to minister. Ministering prophetically is obeying God and serving His children in love. Why would God harshly judge anyone trying to obey Him and help His children? What parent would be harsh and critical with a child who made an innocent mistake while trying to help a sibling?

Jesus tried to help His disciples see this truth as well.

"Now suppose one of you fathers is asked by his son for a fish; he will not give him a snake instead of a fish, will he?

"Or if he is asked for an egg, he will not give him a scorpion, will he?

"If you then, being evil, know how to give good gifts to your children, how much more shall your heavenly Father give the Holy Spirit to those who ask Him?" (Luke 11:11-13)

As stated previously, this analogy reveals God's heart toward providing us with the spiritual gifts we need to minister to others. But would not this fatherly attitude be exhibited in other ways as well? We do not expect our three-year-olds to be as mature as our teenagers. If we did, we would stunt their development. In the same way, God does not expect instant maturity from us.

No one will mature in ministry if they are not given ample opportunity to try their wings without having to fear harsh judgment for mistakes born of immaturity. We must understand that the Lord not only allows, but *expects* us to make mistakes as we begin in ministry.

Is it possible that more people are making mistakes by *not* moving in faith than by sincere, though immature, efforts to follow God's leading? While He is able to correct our mistakes, we must follow Him and do what He has shown us. If we fail to step out in faith, the people who need our ministry will not be touched. All ministry requires us to walk in faith. I discovered this truth the hard way.

Making Sure It Is God

As I was driving across town to my fiancée's house one day in 1988, the Lord spoke to me and instructed me to go see a friend whom I had not seen in six months. We had been estranged from one another because of a misunderstanding. When the Lord spoke to me, my first response was doubt. I immediately thought to myself, *He won't be home; it's the middle of the day!*

Still doubting he would be there but determined to follow God's leading, I drove to his street. However, I wanted to find some way to make sure this word was from God so I would not be embarrassed by pulling into his driveway only to find that he was not there. If he wasn't there, it would mean I had not heard the Lord and was therefore a false prophet. So I decided to drive by his house first to see if his car was in the driveway. As I drove by, sure enough, his car was there! I rejoiced that I had heard the Lord and went to the end of the cul-de-sac to turn my car around.

As I drove back to his house and pulled into the driveway, I was shocked to see that his car was no longer there. In the three minutes it had taken me to turn my car around, he had left! When his sister answered the doorbell, she told me that he had just left for Bible college.

I never saw him again. Our lives went in two different directions from that point, and we never had the opportunity to be reconciled as the Lord wanted. We were robbed of our reconciliation by my fear of missing God and my misconception that I had no room for error in following His leading.

Crushed by my failure, I forgot about my fiancée and returned home. Convinced that the Lord was done with me forever, I fell on my face in repentance, repeatedly promising Him that I would never fail to follow His voice again. However, the error in my understanding was not corrected, and I was headed for disaster.

Round Two

That same evening, as I was driving through the opposite side of town, the Lord spoke to me again. He told me to go by another friend's house because her Buddhist brother was in town from New York and I was to witness to him. Again, my initial response was doubt. *He won't be there; I'm just making this stuff up*, I reasoned.

Having forgotten the painful lesson earlier in the day, I decided to drive past her house to make sure this word really was from God. Just as the Lord had spoken, his car was there—New York license plate and all. Not thinking about the episode earlier that day, I drove to the street's end to turn around, excited that I had heard from God so clearly. Three minutes later, when I returned to her house, I could see her brother's car pulling out of their street onto the main road. I went to the door and found that he had just left to return to New York. I have never seen him again to this day.

In one day, I had two opportunities to see the power of God released by my obedience to His leading. Instead, I had two dramatic failures—not because I did not hear God correctly, but because I tried to *make sure* it was Him before I obeyed! By trying to make sure it was God, I had not moved in faith and missed the blessing that God had reserved for two people.

I wrongly believed that God did not allow for any mistakes for those who move prophetically. As a result, I became immobilized through fear. There I was, required to obey God's unusual leadings, yet with no liberty to miss the mark in any way. Because of the harsh judgment I thought I was receiving from God, I eventually proclaimed, "I will never prophesy to another living creature!"

The Mercy of God

After these and other mistakes, I put all prophetic ministry on the shelf for about eighteen months. During that time, God began to teach me about His mercy, something I badly needed to understand. As I learned about the depth of His love for me, I gradually became bolder in stepping out again in faith. He also placed me in relationships with more mature believers who could disciple me and help me as I grew in understanding about how to function in my spiritual gifts.

The idea that God expects perfection from us is unbiblical. God always provides *for us* what He expects *from us* (see Genesis 22:8-14). He is not expecting instant maturity, but He does expect us to grow into maturity. God wants us to eventually walk in all of His fullness, but this will only come as we are rooted and grounded in His love. Paul prayed this for the believers in Ephesus:

> **so that Christ may dwell in your hearts through faith; and that you, being rooted and grounded in love,**
>
> **may be able to comprehend with all the saints what is the breadth and length and height and depth,**
>
> **and to know the love of Christ which surpasses knowledge, that you may be filled up to all the fulness of God (Ephesians 3:17-19).**

If we do not understand the mercy of God, we will end up missing what God has for us and others. On the other hand, as we become rooted and grounded in His love, we receive greater fullness from God. As we grow in and receive His love, He is able to release greater ministry through us.

We must faithfully serve Him in difficult endeavors, confident in His mercy toward us. Like every person of faith before us, we must launch out, believing in faith what God speaks to us.

God's Method of Confirmation

The Lord does have a method by which He confirms prophetic words and words of direction. We find this mentioned in Exodus 3. However, it may not be the way we *want* Him to confirm things. In this chapter, we find the account of God calling Moses to deliver the Israelites from their Egyptian bondage. Moses had been following sheep around for the past forty years when God suddenly called him into ministry.

God told Moses to approach Pharaoh, ruler of the greatest civilization on earth at that time, and demand that he release his slave labor force (all 1.2 million of them) so they could worship God in the wilderness. Moses, full of self-doubt, tells the Lord that he is not able to accomplish this task. The Lord then encourages Moses and gives him a sign:

> **But Moses said to God, "Who am I, that I should go to Pharaoh, and that I should bring the sons of Israel out of Egypt?"**
>
> **And He said, "Certainly I will be with you, and this shall be the sign to you that it is I who have sent you: when you have brought the people out of Egypt, you shall worship God at this mountain" (Exodus 3:11-12).**

In effect, God told Moses, "This is a sign to you that I have sent you to deliver over a million slaves from their bondage. After you have done it, you will worship Me on this mountain." In other words, "After you've done what I've told you to do, you will know that it was Me who told you to do it!"

Though this method of confirmation may not do much to alleviate our fears, it is often the only way God shows that His word of direction to us is really from Him. When we obey God and step out in faith and the situation works out, then we know that it really was God.

THEN I KNEW

Consider the great prophet Jeremiah. At the risk of his life, he was willing to prophesy a hard word to the king of Israel. He stood against false prophets and prophesied the true, but unpopular, word of God. Surely he must have immediately recognized when God spoke to him. However, if we examine Scripture more closely, we may find differently:

> **And Jeremiah said, "The word of the LORD came to me, saying,**
>
> **'Behold, Hanamel the son of Shallum your uncle is coming to you, saying, "Buy for yourself my field which is at Anathoth, for you have the right of redemption to buy it."**
>
> **"Then Hanamel my uncle's son came to me in the court of the guard according to the word of the LORD, and said to me, 'Buy my field, please, that is at Anathoth, which is in the land of Benjamin; for you have the right of possession and the redemption is yours; buy it for yourself.'** *Then* **I knew that this was the word of the LORD"** **(Jeremiah 32:6-8).**

When the word God had spoken to him came to pass, *then* Jeremiah knew that it was the Lord! When we read that the word of the Lord came to the Old Testament prophets, we envision much more dramatic circumstances than what usually happened. We think of thundering voices, wheels within wheels, four living creatures, and angelic visitations. However, much of what they received prophetically was on a lower level of revelation. Sometimes they did not know that a word was from the Lord until it came to pass.

The Necessity of Faith

We need to recognize that every aspect of God's work requires us to walk in faith. Prophetic ministry is no different. While it is awesome to witness someone moving in dramatic levels of prophetic ministry, when we are the vessels the Lord is using, we may at first experience fear instead of euphoria. Prophesying, like any ministry, is a step of faith that usually requires us to get past our feelings and our fears.

Since prophetic ministry is telling people things that we do not know by our own knowledge, it is like walking on water every time we do it. If we are insecure in the Lord's willingness to cover us, we will struggle as we give prophetic words.

Faith and humility are two primary requirements for prophetic ministry. There are two ways you can circumvent these requirements: Do not prophesy at all or cheat when you do. Cheating is prophesying things you already know in the natural, which is a characteristic of false prophets. While most believers avoid this temptation, many fall to the first. They do not prophesy because they are afraid of making mistakes.

However, mistakes are not optional. Although no one enjoys the process, the way most of us learn is through trial and error. When we try something new, we will make errors. This is the nature of life and ministry. If we are unwilling to function at an immature level of prophetic ministry, we will probably never walk in mature prophetic ministry. We must crawl before we walk.

BEGINNING REVELATION

When we first begin, we usually start out with prophetic ministry that is not spectacular. But we must not despise the day of small beginnings. If we will only give the revelation, God is able to profoundly touch people through the smallest and simplest prophetic revelations.

Several years ago, I held some prophetic training classes in a small town in another state. After some basic instruction about the prophetic gifts to a group of about fifty people, I released them to minister to someone in the meeting. A young lady from a nearby town volunteered to receive prophetic ministry from the others.

After we prayed for the Lord to give us words for her, people began sharing what the Lord had given them. Many relayed Scripture verses or visions that were very encouraging to her. The majority of them spoke directly to her present situation, even though none of the people knew her. At the end of our ministry time, a man in the back said he had received a picture, but was unsure what it meant. He said simply that he had seen a picture of a kangaroo while praying.

Immediately, the entire group erupted in laughter at this picture, because it seemed out of place. People began making jokes about kangaroos and were talking loudly among themselves while the man sat back in his chair somewhat embarrassed by the reaction.

Trying to restore some semblance of order, I turned to the lady and asked if she had ever been to Australia. She replied that she had been a missionary in Australia for two years and had lived on a ranch there. She reported that the owner of the ranch had a pet kangaroo that would follow her around everywhere she went. She was back in the United States now, looking for direction from the Lord. A hush came over the crowd as the fear of God fell in the room.

This simple prophetic word propelled her into quite a journey over the next eighteen months. Encouraged by the "kangaroo word," she moved across the country to attend a ministry training school, less than one month after receiving the word. Two months later, a prophetic minister visiting the school called her out at a meeting and spoke to her about a calling to Australia and New Zealand.

One month later, another minister visiting the school gave her a similar word. Upon graduation, she was invited to work with one of the strongest ministries in New Zealand. She now lives there, ministering in New Zealand, Australia, and throughout Asia. She points back to a simple word at a small meeting, in a small town, as the catalyst that put her in the geographic will of God more than 10,000 miles away.

There are several simple but profound principles in this story. First, *anything worth doing is worth doing poorly.* While this is offensive to perfectionists, it is a powerful truth. We start where we are and grow from there. Some people want to be excellent in ministry before they ever begin ministering! But that's not how it works.

What musicians become skilled with their instruments without making thousands of mistakes as they learn how to play? The answer is none. Then why do we expect people just beginning to move in prophetic gifts to do everything perfectly from the start? We must be willing to do it poorly before we can do it with excellence. The key is to just get started. The sooner we start, the quicker we can become excellent.

The man who gave the kangaroo word started in a weak fashion because he did not have an interpretation, just a simple picture. From that simple beginning, he has progressed remarkably. One of the last times I saw him minister prophetically was two years after the kangaroo word. By then, his confidence had blossomed and his accuracy in prophecy was amazing. He would never have matured in his gifts, however, without the freedom to "try his wings" in a safe environment with no fear of being labeled a false prophet if he failed.

There is another important lesson in this example. This man did not attempt to create an interpretation of the picture he saw; he simply shared what God gave him. Instead of diluting a valid word from God with his own interpretation, he allowed God to fill in the blanks. *The one word God speaks is more powerful than a thousand that we can speak on our own.* Though the mental picture he saw seemed foolish, God supplied the interpretation through someone else. Through this word many lives were changed forever.

INCOMPLETE REVELATION

Another obstacle that some experience as they begin to prophesy is *incomplete revelation.* While in France for a conference, I received a vision one night immediately after retiring to bed. I saw a woman with red hair wearing an Australian hat on her head. I immediately thought, "Some woman needs an Australian covering (husband)," but I did not know whom this was for. I turned my reading lamp back on and wrote the vision down. When I turned the lamp on, a team member who was traveling with me also received something from the Lord and wrote it down. We did not discuss the words that we had received.

The next day this team member began ministering to the man who was driving us to lunch. He encouraged this man, who was an evangelist, that the Lord was for him and that this year would be better than the last. The driver thanked my friend and began to describe his deep and painful experience during the last year. He explained that he had been engaged to a girl from Australia, but that they had decided not to get married. Although he felt this was from the Lord, it had been incredibly painful to endure and he had almost left the ministry.

I immediately told him my vision about the girl with the Australian hat from the night before. My friend then told the man that he had received the word of encouragement for him at the same time I received the vision! We admitted to him that we could not explain everything about his situation, and we did not receive any further insights. Our new friend still had many unanswered questions because our revelation was incomplete.

The next day as we entered the conference hall, I saw this evangelist standing across the room, and I immediately saw a transformation in him. I turned to my friend and said, "God has healed the crack that was causing him to leak. Look, he's fatter in the Spirit today!" When I said this, my friend looked stunned. He told me that the previous day, a woman had come to him with a vision she had received for this evangelist. In it she saw him as a clay vessel with a crack that was causing him to leak. The crack was a wound in his spirit.

God confirmed to us that this man had been healed through what we had considered incomplete revelation. Regardless of how incomplete our revelation was, God had healed him. *Incomplete revelation still has power to heal.* As we mature in prophetic ministry, we must never disregard what God gives us, even when it is incomplete. We should pursue the Lord for more revelation, but if we do not receive any more, we should still give what we have.

GENERAL REVELATION

Another area that shuts down inexperienced people is receiving very *general revelation.* Because we are often looking for profoundly specific words, we sometimes reject the general revelation that God is giving us.

This was true in the case of a good friend of mine named Carl. He met the Lord as a result of what most people would consider a very general prophetic revelation. He had become very successful in business before he was thirty years old, only to see it all crumble before his eyes. While driving to work one day, he saw a billboard advertising a competitor's business which was thriving. Although he did not know the Lord, Carl began questioning God as to why his business was failing even though he was honest, and his competitor's business was thriving, although he was corrupt.

Immediately, God showed my friend all of the times He had tried to draw him to Himself and how often he had rejected the Lord. He broke down emotionally and began to weep in his car. Deeply convicted, he cried out in his distress, "God have I gotten so far from You that I can never get back to You?" He wept uncontrollably during the remainder of his drive and for thirty minutes after arriving at his office.

While trying to regain his composure, a business acquaintance called and left an urgent message for Carl to call him at home. He called the gentleman and finally reached him on his car phone. This man explained to my friend that he was a Christian and often prayed for my friend and his family. He said that during his morning run, the Lord had reminded him of my friend. He then prayed for Carl as he ran. After this gentleman finished his run, the Lord told him to call my friend and tell him that "he had not gotten so far from God that he could never get back to Him." My friend had a profound encounter with the Lord as a result.

Many are looking for spectacular prophetic revelation and dismiss the general revelation. Saying to someone, "You haven't gotten so far from God that you can never come back," may not seem like a high-level revelation or ministry in our opinion, unless we know that person's situation (and we usually do not when God uses us prophetically). This is a very important concept: *What may sound general to us is often extremely pointed and accurate to the person for whom it is intended.* We cannot judge prophecy before it is given. We must give it first and then let the people we are prophesying to judge it.

There are several other principles that we can see in this example. First, this man obeyed God at the risk of his reputation. He had to push past fear of ridicule or rejection in order to give this word. We must get past these fears if we are to ever be fruitful in prophetic ministry. We will overcome them when we realize that the *obedience which may cause us to look foolish may also bring someone's salvation.*

REJECTED REVELATION

Another area that beginners need to deal with is *rejected revelation.* Often people are more prone to receive a word from someone who has a reputation for being prophetic. While this may not be right, it is a reality. As such, when we begin in prophetic ministry, people may often reject the prophetic words we give to them because they have no previous experience with us. Also, people may not realize that the word is valid and may reject it out of ignorance.

A good example of this occurred during a conference I attended in another country. After the last session, a very kind, young woman asked to speak with me because she believed she had a prophetic word for me. She said that the Lord had told her there was a wound between my wife and me and that she would like to pray for it to be healed.

I thanked her for her willingness to share the word, but told her that there was no wound between my wife and me. In an attempt to encourage her, I told her that I did miss my family since I had a newborn son at home and did not really want to be thousands of miles away from them. I told her she was probably sensing my feelings of missing my family. After encouraging her, I turned to walk away.

Very kindly, she stopped me and asked if she could pray for me anyway. I let her pray for me and then thanked her again for stepping out in faith. When I arrived home, I found that there was a new freshness in my marriage from the moment I stepped over the threshold. There *had* been a wound between my wife and me that neither of us was aware of, but now it was gone. *The Lord healed my marriage through a prophetic word that I rejected.*

Just like this woman, we do not need to worry when our words are not received. They often have power even when they are rejected. God is only asking us to deliver them. We are not responsible to see that they are received. If we will do our part, then He will do the rest.

> Note: If I had told this woman, "No, you cannot pray for me," it would have been wrong for her to persist and pray with me anyway. If I had refused her prayers, I would have missed what God had for me, since my humility and her prayer were part of God's plan. We cannot force people to receive our words. We must simply give them and trust the Holy Spirit to do His part.

Walking on the Water

Our part is easy, unless we begin to analyze it. If we begin reasoning about a word God has given us, we are probably in danger of not giving it. Prophesying is a lot like walking on the water. We are asked to do something that we cannot do. God asks us to tell people things about themselves and their situations that we could not know. This is difficult when we are enslaved to our reason, afraid of failing, or afraid of appearing foolish.

We must be willing to look foolish in order to walk in prophetic gifts. A prophetic word that is not given cannot minister to anyone. We must give what God has given us. I Corinthians 14:3 says that **"one who prophesies *speaks* to men."** We must *speak* to them or they will not benefit from the word. If we stay within the parameters of encouragement, edification, and comfort, we will not make harmful mistakes. The prophetic words we receive for others can bring restoration, healing, and deliverance. Share what God gives you without the fear of being labeled false.

Chapter Seven
ADMINISTRATING PROPHECY

Recognizing when God is speaking and understanding what He is saying are both crucial elements to prophesying accurately. However, knowing how to present a word to someone is also important. We should always endeavor to minister prophetically in a way that honors the Lord *and* His people. Prophecy does not just entail speaking God's mind; it also includes speaking with His *heart*.

While some mistakes in the prophetic are born from immaturity and insecurity, others spring from a lack of instruction about *how* to minister prophetically. In this chapter, we will provide seven parameters for administrating prophecy in the local church. These parameters can help ensure that our words will build and encourage rather than devastate.

1) YOUR LEVEL OF AUTHORITY

Many problems in the prophetic can be eliminated by an understanding of God's plan for authority in the church. One of the greatest concerns among pastors and church leaders is the tendency of some prophetic people to prophesy beyond their realm of authority. In other words, they tend to prophesy about things they should not, or in a way they should not.

In the kingdom of God, authority flows from responsibility. Generally, we only have authority in any area of the church to the degree that we have responsibility for that area. If we do not have responsibility for an area, then we do not have real authority in that area.

Paul touches on this idea when defending his apostleship to the Corinthians in his second letter to them.

But we will not boast of things without our measure, but according to the *measure of the rule* which God hath distributed to us, a measure to reach even unto you (II Corinthians 10:13 KJV).

Paul described the authority that he had with the Corinthians as **"the measure of the rule"** which God had distributed to him. This measure of authority came because Paul had birthed this church and was still responsible for it before God.

Consider this analogy. If my next door neighbor comes into my yard, sees my children doing something that he does not like, and then disciplines my children, he is out of order. Even though he is an adult, he has no authority to discipline my children because he has no responsibility for them. Instead of disciplining my children, he could alert me to the problems he has seen and allow me to handle it. Since I am responsible for them, I have authority over them.

However, if I ask my neighbor to care for my children while I am out of town for two days, I will give him limited authority to discipline my children during that time frame because he is responsible for them during those two days. I have given him authority over my children because I have asked him to be responsible for them.

"At Large" Authority

Many problems arise when people think they have an "at large" authority in the church because they are prophetic and can see problems. They believe this gives them authority to speak into any situation for which they receive prophetic insight. This is not the case.

If you have no responsibility in a local congregation, then you have no real authority in that congregation. As a pastor in our local congregation, I have authority in our congregation since I have responsibility for it (see Hebrews 13:17). However, when I travel to minister to other congregations, I have no real authority since I have no responsibility for them.

When I minister in different congregations, the Lord will often give me prophetic revelation identifying future leaders or people who are causing difficulty. This comes by revelation, not by any experience I have with them. Although the Lord speaks to me about these issues, I will not prophesy or address them publicly because it is not my responsibility to appoint elders or to correct those causing trouble in these congregations. The leadership which God has established in that local congregation is responsible for these issues. For me to address these problems directly would be a violation of their God-given authority over that congregation.

A PRACTICAL EXAMPLE

During one of my first ministry trips outside our congregation, the Lord prophetically revealed to me during worship that a certain man was being considered for a position as an elder in that congregation. Through the discernment of spirits, I saw the specific area of his intended function as an elder and that he was to be appointed as elder within the next six months. He also showed me that this man's wife was a strong woman whose strength had been misinterpreted as control by some in the congregation. This misunderstanding was hindering the pastor from appointing the man as an elder.

Instead of giving this word to the couple publicly in the meeting, I relayed it later to the pastor. He was amazed by the revelation and thankful because he had been unsure of what to do in this situation. He could now move forward in confidence with this man's appointment as an elder because of the prophetic revelation and confirmation. I advised the pastor to still wait until he was comfortable with this situation and not to act too quickly on my word.

Why did I not give this word publicly to the couple? Would it not have been more powerful for everyone to see God speak prophetically through me by identifying this couple, explaining the situation, and giving the word of wisdom? Listed below are several reasons why it was proper to give this word privately to the leaders of this congregation, instead of publicly to the couple.

1. I was not responsible to appoint elders in that congregation; the pastor and leadership team were the ones with that authority. What could have transpired if I had given that word publicly? Maybe some of the people would have agreed and the leadership team would have disagreed. I could have easily created a serious problem by sharing this revelation with those who were not responsible.

2. Since it was not yet time for the man to become an elder, my word given publicly could have released impatience in the man and caused difficulty in his relationship with the leadership team. Given publicly, this word could have actually kept the

man from becoming an elder by causing him to set his heart on this position in a wrong way.

3. I could have been wrong. If I gave this word publicly, the entire congregation would have been responsible to judge it; many of them may not have been mature enough to do this. However, since I gave the word privately to the pastor and other elders who were responsible, they could judge the word privately and do what they deemed correct. They were responsible to lead and oversee that congregation, not me.

The potential risk of giving this word publicly to the congregation far outweighed the benefit. Some of you may think, "But it would be dramatic and powerful to give a word like this publically." While that may be true, I am not interested in being dramatic and powerful—I want to be wise and effective. There is a temptation to perform our ministry in a way that builds our reputation at the expense of building the people. Do not do it.

The authority that I do have in these situations is a *referent authority.* Although not a legal authority, I have a type of authority with the pastors because they trust me and my ministry. This is an authority based on friendship and respect, not a real authority. As such, I only offer my revelation to them as a friend and not an overseer in their lives.

A WARNING

Authority in the church does not come from revelation; it comes from responsibility. If the leadership of your congregation does not receive your revelation or chooses to wait before using it, that is their prerogative. You should not go to someone else in the congregation to discuss your revelation if the leadership does not agree with you or does not act on your insight. If you do this, you have stepped outside of God's authority structure and will probably bring division, instead of unity to the church.

Understanding our level of authority also determines how we approach someone. If I receive a word for someone who is a friend, I present the revelation to them as a friend. If I receive a word for someone who is an authority in my life, I present it humbly, entreating them as an elder. If I receive a word for someone for whom I have responsibility as their pastor, I will present it in that vein as well. Our level of authority dictates how and with whom we share our revelation.

2) YOUR LEVEL OF REVELATION

In addition to understanding our level of authority, we also need to prophesy according to our *level of revelation.* Because those to whom we minister are responsible to judge prophecy, we should communicate to them the level on which we received our revelation when we prophesy to them.

As previously stated, there are three basic components to any prophetic word: the *revelation*, the *interpretation*, and the *application*. There are also many different levels of revelation ranging from low level to high level which were defined in Chapter Three.

Whenever we present a word as coming on a higher level than we actually received it, we are misleading people as to how strongly God is speaking to them. If we receive an impression, which is a valid type of revelation, yet we tell someone that "God spoke to me about you," we have prophesied inaccurately. Conversely, if God speaks audibly to us, we should tell people exactly that: "God spoke to me." If an angel appears to you and gives you a message for someone, we should tell them that as well.

It is important to present revelation on the same level we receive it. One of the most trusted positions during biblical times was that of an ambassador. The person chosen for this job was to represent in word, attitude, and action the king or authority sending them. So it is with us. As we minister prophetically, we must also be those who do not misrepresent the Lord, but speak even as it was spoken to us.

3) YOUR LEVEL OF UNDERSTANDING

We must also prophesy according to our *level of understanding*. I have seen many believers who, as they begin to move prophetically, receive the slightest impression or the gentlest vision and attempt to prophesy far beyond their level of understanding. Instead of simply reporting what they feel or see from the Lord, they attempt to give a very detailed prophetic message beyond their understanding.

Using the example from the last chapter of the man who received a simple picture of a kangaroo, let me illustrate this point. When my friend simply gave this seemingly insignificant picture which he did not understand, God gave someone else the interpretation, and the ministry was powerful. In fact, what appeared weak was a very specific word and propelled the person receiving it into the geographic will of God for her life, 10,000 miles away!

If this gentleman had been uncomfortable sharing something he did not completely understand, he could have made a significant blunder. If he had felt it necessary to concoct an interpretation, he would have destroyed the power of this revelation. If we do not receive an interpretation, we should not create one! If we "muddy the waters" for people by prophesying beyond our level of understanding, it makes it harder for them to hear the Lord than if we had only given what we had received and stopped there.

As another example of this, I was once asked to minister prophetically to a group of people during a conference. While praying for someone, I received a clear vision of a tuning fork. The Lord then showed me this man's calling and some things that happened when he was a child which were hindering him. While I was confident the vision of the tuning fork was important, I was unsure of what it represented, and so I quickly formulated my own interpretation.

As I began ministering to him, I said that I had received a vision of a tuning fork. Before I could continue with "my interpretation," the man reacted by excitedly exclaiming that he made his living as a piano tuner. Without missing a beat, I aborted "my interpretation" and simply gave him the other items the Lord had shown me. He was deeply touched by God and released from those things which had been hindering him.

Had he not interrupted me, I would have gone beyond what I had received to a "created" interpretation. If so, this man would probably not have had such a powerful encounter with the Lord. In fact, he probably would have walked away confused instead of encouraged and strengthened. The Lord protected him from my error of going beyond my understanding. It was better to give the little that God had given me than for me to add to it beyond my understanding.

4) YOUR LEVEL OF FAITH

Another parameter to abide by when prophesying is to not go beyond our *level of faith*. Paul exhorts us to this end in his Epistle to the Roman Christians.

And since we have gifts that differ according to the grace given to us, let each exercise them accordingly: if prophecy, according to the proportion of his faith (Romans 12:6).

There are two different issues that we need to understand regarding ministering according to our level of faith. First, although God may use us prophetically on any level He chooses, we generally grow gradually in any area of grace. We should be comfortable to begin moving prophetically in a manner consistent with our faith. As a general rule, we should probably not expect God to give us the intimate details of someone's life history when we first begin ministering prophetically. We will probably begin on a decidedly lower level and this is okay.

Another issue that we need to consider in prophesying according to our level of faith is that we should always prophesy *in faith*. For example, if God shows you through a word of knowledge that someone is sick, then we should not simply tell them, "The Lord has shown me that you have an illness" and leave it at that. We must understand God's heart and that He desires to heal. We then can pray in faith and see people healed of their diseases.

Several years ago, I received a powerful revelation for a friend. I had written in my appointment calendar to cancel an appointment with him for the next day. Later in the day, while checking my "To Do" list, I looked at my calendar and was amazed at what I saw.

Upon completing my tasks, my habit is to put a line through them on my calendar to avoid overlooking anything. When I looked at my planner, the only thing without a line through it was my note to call my friend. As I looked at the message, it no longer said "cancel," but "cancer." I shook my head and looked again and saw his name with the word "cancer" written beside it. I looked again, and it now read "cancel."

As I sought the Lord about this, He spoke to me. "The enemy is trying to convince Alan that the cancer has returned." Prior to meeting him several years earlier, my friend had been diagnosed with lung cancer. Being trained in a Christian group that did not believe God heals or performs miracles today, he did not seek the Lord for healing. However, the Lord appeared to him in his living room one day, rebuked him for his pride, and healed him of the cancer (he has the "before and after" x-rays that verify his healing).

When I called to discuss what the Lord had revealed to me, his answering machine picked up, so I simply canceled our appointment. Not wanting to leave a word of this nature on his answering machine, I made a mental note to call him later. To my discredit, I forgot to call him.

Two weeks later, I was returning to Charlotte from a trip with a co-worker and found myself driving on the very road where my friend lived. I began sharing what the Lord had shown me, and we decided to stop and minister to him.

When I pulled into his driveway, his wife was returning to their house from another building on their property. I asked her where her husband was. She said that he had been sick and was inside the house. I immediately said to her, "He thinks the cancer is back, doesn't he?" Shocked, she acknowledged this was true.

As we entered his house, my friend emerged from his bedroom, looking very haggard. Indeed he had been coughing for about ten days and felt much like he did before the Lord had healed him of cancer years previously. If I had not clearly heard the Lord expose the enemy's deception of trying to convince him that the cancer was back, I too would have been deceived. He looked very much like a man deep in the throes of cancer.

I explained to him what I had received, and my friend and I prayed for him, standing with him against this lie of the enemy and praying for his health. God gave us other prophetic insight about this situation as we prayed. The next week he had a biopsy and the doctors discovered a benign tumor in his lung where the cancerous tumor had disappeared years before. They were able to remove it, and he is as healthy as the proverbial horse today.

The doctors were amazed because they had never seen nor even heard in any medical research of a benign tumor of this sort located in someone's lung. Our conclusion was that if we had not received this clear word from the Lord and broken any agreement with the enemy's plan, the tumor would have been cancerous. If I had operated from a foundation of fear, instead of faith, I could have been used by the enemy to agree with his purposes for my friend's life, instead of God's. We must prophesy in faith!

We must remember that God speaks prophetically to change existing situations and to preempt the plans of Satan. We must never fall into the trap of prophesying the enemy's plan as God's purpose. Prophesying in faith is simply having confidence in God and His mercy and prophesying accordingly.

5) MITIGATED BY LOVE

And if I have the gift of prophecy, and know all mysteries and all knowledge; and if I have all faith, so as to remove mountains, but do not have love, I am nothing (I Corinthians 13:2).

While prophecy entails bringing a message *from* God, we must also never forget we are speaking *to* His children. We should always minister prophetically, motivated by God's love. God probably does not appreciate anyone being harsh with His children.

Some of our traditional understandings about prophets and prophetic ministry are definitely askew. While many envision prophets as angry men, pronouncing judgment on the multitudes, this ministry should be motivated by God's love just as all the other ministries are.

In Revelation 19:10, John records that **"the testimony of Jesus is the spirit of prophecy."** The witness of Jesus is God's sacrificial love for mankind, and the motivating force of prophecy, therefore, is God's love (the next chapter of this book deals more extensively with this subject). Whenever we prophesy, it should reveal God's loving nature.

Some people have communicated God's word while miscommunicating His heart. God does not want to destroy people through the gift of prophecy—He desires to build them. As Paul spoke in his first letter to the Corinthians, **"love builds up" (see I Corinthians 8:1 NIV).** As we minister prophetically in love, people will be built up, not destroyed.

6) IMPART HOPE

At the end of his discourse on love in I Corinthians 13, Paul states that there are three eternal virtues: faith, hope, and love. If we want our ministry to the body of Christ to be eternal in nature, it should contain each of these qualities. Any prophetic word that we give should not only be given in faith, motivated by love, but it should also impart hope.

Even a cursory glance at the Old Testament shows that God is all too willing to delay or cancel judgment if people change their behavior. Indeed, that is much of the purpose of prophecy. Consider this revelation of God's heart: **"For I have no pleasure in the death of anyone who dies," declares the Lord GOD. "Therefore, repent and live" (Ezekiel 18:32).**

From His dealings with Nineveh to Ahab, we see that God is merciful as well as just. He is gracious and long-suffering, desiring that all men walk according to His ways that He might bless them. We must understand that God always gives hope. We must also minister hope as we minister prophetically.

7) MINISTER IN HUMILITY

Lastly, we must minister prophetically from a position of humility. When we minister to anyone, we are not ministering from a "blank page." We need to understand that many who went before us prophetically have made mistakes by misrepresenting God's heart. It is incumbent upon us to recover the spirit of prophecy, which is love expressed with humility.

If we use Isaiah's prophecy and description of Christ as our model for ministry, we will not only administrate prophecy correctly, but we will bring healing to those who have been wounded through improper prophetic ministry done in the past.

> **"Behold, My Servant, whom I uphold; My chosen one in whom My soul delights. I have put My Spirit upon Him; He will bring forth justice to the nations.**
>
> **"He will not cry out or raise His voice, nor make His voice heard in the street.**
>
> **"A bruised reed He will not break, and a dimly burning wick He will not extinguish; He will faithfully bring forth justice" (Isaiah 42:1-3).**

To not break a bruised reed means we are not rough with those whose lives have been devastated in the past. To not extinguish the dimly burning wick means we will not put out the weakly burning embers, which are the only remainder of what was once their spiritual life. To be like Jesus, we must prophesy life to those who are at even the lowest point, not simply tell them how far they have fallen.

PRACTICAL HUMILITY

In a practical way, I try to never intimidate anyone in a ministry situation. If someone is seated before me and I begin to prophesy to them, I do not stand over them and deliver my word. I kneel in front of them, positioning myself lower than them, so that they do not feel intimidated or placed in a subservient position. I also generally smile when I prophesy to them, because I want to communicate God's love to them in every way possible.

I also never assume that I have the right to lay my hands on someone and pray for them. A significant portion of our society has experienced either verbal, physical, or sexual abuse, and we want to bring healing to these through an expression of the Lord's gentleness and humility. We always ask permission from someone before we pray or lay hands on them, letting them know that they are in charge and must give us permission to minister to them. Do not assume this right—ask for it.

A WAY OF LIFE

Although we must study to add these understandings to our lives, we cannot simply create a *prophetic checklist* of these different items and filter each prophetic word that we receive through it. They must become part of the prophetic life with God to which each of us is called. As they become a part of our lives, we will be used by God in increasing measures of His prophetic grace.

Chapter Eight

RECOVERING THE SPIRIT OF PROPHECY

There is a significant amount of misunderstanding concerning prophets and their ministry. Many people believe the prophetic ministry is comprised almost exclusively of angry people thundering God's judgments. In fact, one pastor recently commented to me, "It is dangerous to have the prophetic ministry in a church." Although I disagree with this statement, I understand the concern and frustration behind it. Because of misunderstandings about the prophetic ministry and mistakes by some who have functioned prophetically, many people are afraid of the prophetic.

This presents an important series of questions for us. Are prophetic people, by virtue of their calling, critical, angry, and uncompassionate? If you are prophetic, are you supposed to be angry and unloving by nature? If you are loving and caring, are you less prophetic than the prophets listed in the Bible? Or do we possess serious misunderstandings about prophets and the prophetic ministry?

As previously stated, this book is not intended as a treatise on the office of a prophet. However, for the purpose of understanding and recovering the spirit of prophecy, we will examine the lives and function of some biblical prophets.

OUR VIEW IS LIMITED

Many of our general concepts about those called to prophetic ministry are inaccurate at best—some are dangerous. Many of these wrong ideas are founded upon a very limited view of a few Old Testament prophets, instead of a comprehensive overview of them all.

In many cases, we have been so enamored by Old Covenant prophets and their exploits, that we considered their character flaws as "prophetic traits." Instead of recognizing that their attitudes were wrong, we have created reasons and excuses for them. This has arisen from two basic problems. First, our understanding of God's heart has been less than accurate. In spite of the Scriptures to the contrary, many still believe that God is angry, impatient, and easily provoked. As such, we have represented Him this way through our prophetic ministry.

Second, we have had difficulty reconciling the fact that biblical prophets moved in such power and revelation while still having sinful attitudes. Because many have not understood God allowing such power and revelation to be released through weak and imperfect vessels, we have believed that prophets were supposed to be harsh and judgmental. Otherwise, if they were wrong in their attitudes, how could God have used them so powerfully?

One sign of maturity is the ability to understand that revelation and power demonstrated through a person is not necessarily an endorsement of their attitudes. The biblical prophets who represented the Lord as harsh and unforgiving were wrong, and God did hold them accountable for their sinfulness.

EXPANDING OUR VIEW

Not all Old Covenant prophets were wrathful and harsh. We need to broaden our view of the prophets and reexamine our existing prophetic "role models," to accurately understand God's heart for the prophetic ministry.

Paul writes in I Corinthians 14:3 that prophecy is for encouragement, building one another up, and comforting one another. However, most of our Old Testament models do not meet these criteria and neither do many of those in our personal experience. So how do we reconcile this?

We need to recognize that our attempt to define prophetic ministry by our limited encounters with a few individuals is like the parable of four blind men and an elephant. Each man attempted to define it solely from the one part that he had touched. In attempting to recreate the whole from a single part, we have created a gross caricature of this ministry that betrays the very spirit behind it.

THE DANGER OF LOOKING AT A MAN

Rick Joyner has commented that a significant problem in the church is our tendency to judge any group by its most extreme elements. This has definitely happened with the prophetic ministry. When we think of a prophet, Elijah often springs to mind. We see him engaged in spiritual warfare on Mt. Carmel, calling an apostate nation to repentance. We see a solitary figure calmly praying and God answering by fire. We see him slaying the false prophets in an expression of God's judgment. When we think of the prophetic, we think of power, miracles, and holiness.

Elijah and other prophets cut imposing figures and have quite naturally become our standard for prophetic ministry. But this presents a serious danger if we do not understand a very basic principle of ministry. God may infuse a person's words with His power without simultaneously endorsing his attitude. We must separate the exploits of the prophets from their wrong attitudes so that our standard of this ministry will be accurate.

Issuing spiritual ultimatums was not the exclusive prophetic function. Many Old Covenant prophets functioned as counselors to Israel's kings; some even gave God's counsel to pagan kings. Not all of the Old Testament prophets harshly treated those around them. As we examine the wider spectrum of prophets, our understanding of this ministry and the spirit behind it will broaden as well.

The Elijah Model

For most people, Elijah represents the highest model of prophetic ministry. He was uncompromising in his resistance against idolatry in Israel. He stood boldly before the worst king in Israel's history and declared the word of God without fear or compromise. He proclaimed there would be no rain except at his word, and there was no rain for three years (see I Kings 17:1). He also single-handedly rid Israel of 850 false prophets in one encounter (see I Kings 18:19). He is a good example of faith and courage.

However, the Scriptures say that he was a man of human frailties like us (see James 5:17). He was lacking in compassion, patience, and a redemptive heart. Paul writes in Romans 11:2-3 that Elijah actually interceded against Israel in his despair and anger. He cried out for God to judge and deal harshly with them.

He also apparently misjudged Obadiah who, the Bible says, feared God greatly (see I Kings 18:3). Additionally, Elijah was self-willed, not completing the assignments given to him by God, but leaving them to his successor (see I Kings 19:15-16). While we can admire his faith and courage, he did not embody the spirit of the New Testament prophet and prophecy.

TRUE PROPHETS WHO HELPED AHAB

For those who hold Elijah to be the proto-prophet, it is enlightening to examine the other prophets of his day. On three separate occasions, God sent prophets other than Elijah to direct and inspire Ahab during battles (see I Kings 20:13-28). Many today, with a narrow understanding of the prophetic ministry, cannot imagine God sending prophets to help and encourage Ahab, who had led Israel into idolatry.

However, even under the Old Covenant with Israel's worst king, prophets were called to help and encourage the one in leadership. They functioned in this capacity because they were motivated by God who is patient and long-suffering.

They did not encourage sin, but they did bring strength and help during times of battle and in preparation against the enemies of God. If this was the case under the Old Covenant, how much more redemptive should the prophetic ministry be under the New Covenant?

When Ahab disobeyed God's command, another prophet came and rebuked him for not heeding the Lord (see I Kings 20:41-43). Later, when Elijah brought warning of God's judgment, Ahab repented. Remarkably, God instructed Elijah to mark how Ahab humbled himself (see I Kings 21:17-29). God saw Ahab's repentance and delayed the judgment coming to his house. God was trying to teach Elijah about His heart to save, redeem, and forgive so that the prophet would reflect God's nature which rejoices in mercy, not judgment.

In many cases, prophets today need to hear God's instruction to Elijah and see how patient He is with His people. He is longing to show His mercy and will quickly move on behalf of someone who takes one step of repentance, no matter how small (see Luke 15:17-23).

Which Spirit Are You?

Another damaging concept of prophets also comes from the life of Elijah. After being confronted by Elijah for his idolatry, Ahaziah, king of Israel, sent a captain with fifty men to bring Elijah to his palace. As they approached Elijah and demanded that he come with them, he called down fire from heaven and the soldiers were killed. Another captain with his fifty men were dispatched to bring Elijah back and were likewise consumed as well (see II Kings 1:9-12).

Taking this story to heart and ignoring Jesus' command to love our enemies has led some to believe that prophets are exempt from the fruit of the Spirit and the walk of love. Having been molded by this wrong concept, some prophetic people are quick to call down judgment whenever they are threatened or rebuffed. In fact, some of Jesus' disciples held this wrong concept as well.

When traveling to Jerusalem, Jesus would have passed through Samaria, but the Samaritans would not allow him into their country (see Luke 9:51-56). His disciples, enraged by this insult, asked Jesus, **"Do you want us to call fire down from heaven to destroy them?" (see Luke 9:54 NIV)** They did not ask *Him* to do it; they asked if He wanted *them* to do it for Him!

The previous day, these same disciples did not offer to deliver a young demon-possessed child. They were not nearly as motivated by love as they were by anger. Jesus' reply is a rebuke to all who are mistaken about the spirit of prophecy today: **"You do not know what kind of spirit you are of, for the Son of Man did not come to destroy men's lives, but to save them" (see Luke 9:55-56).** His disciples did not realize that love, not anger, was the true prophetic motivation.

Being prophetic means we should not only hear God's words, but we should have His nature as well. If we want to be truly prophetic, we must have the spirit of prophecy which is the testimony of Jesus (see Revelation 19:10). The testimony of Jesus, or His witness, is God's redeeming love for mankind. Remember, **"God is love" (see I John 4:8, 16).**

God's love is not sloppy, gushing, or sentimental. God's love is not afraid to speak truth, but it is not anxious to judge either. In fact, the ability to speak the truth motivated by love is difficult and is a mark of Christian maturity (see Ephesians 4:15). If our motivation is anger, rooted in pride, we will be prone to quickly offer judgment instead of patiently interceding for mercy.

JUDGMENT OR GRACE?

One prophetic friend learned this lesson the hard way. A powerful prophet with an extremely accurate ministry once prophesied judgment upon a group of pastors for a period of five minutes, reacting in anger to their sinful attitude. The Lord rebuked him for speaking from his own anger and declared that he would be sick for five months—one month for every minute of judgment that he prophesied on God's people. He quickly learned what spirit he was of and did not repeat this mistake.

Judging is much too easy and can be rooted in our carnality. To truly prophesy the life and hope necessary to change a situation, requires God's touch. If we offer judgment without offering hope, it is probably because we are still operating from our carnal minds, not the Holy Spirit. The Holy Spirit not only knows what is wrong in a situation; He knows how to help make it right because He is the Helper.

The Jonah Model

The Jonah model is an updated version of the Elijah model. God had instructed him to go to the Assyrians, but Jonah did not want to help them because they were Israel's enemies. Instead, he boarded a ship heading in the opposite direction. When God sent a storm because of Jonah's presence on their ship, the heathen sailors were more spiritually sensitive than Jonah. Recognizing the spiritual nature of the storm, they prayed to their idols and inquired why this storm had been sent.

When it was discovered that Jonah was to blame, these idol worshipers were unwilling to sacrifice his life for theirs. They rowed with all their might, at their own risk, to save Jonah. Finally, seeing there was no other hope but to obey Jonah's word and throw him overboard, they did. Consider that these pagans had more compassion for someone who brought judgment on them, than the man of God who claimed to understand God's goodness and mercy (see Jonah 4:2).

Jonah may have theologically understood God's love, but he did not possess very much of it. He was possibly the most stubborn prophet on record. It took three days and three nights in a fish's belly before he humbled himself and repented of his sin! (see Jonah 1; 2:1) I think I would have repented the moment I was thrown overboard, and if not at that moment, then the instant a fish swallowed me.

When he was restored to dry land, the Lord once again spoke to him, sending him to Nineveh. This time Jonah went and declared, **"Yet forty days, and Nineveh shall be overthrown" (see Jonah 3:4 KJV).** When the entire city repented to the degree that everyone from the king to the cattle was wearing sackcloth and ashes, God canceled the judgment against them. Jonah, having no love for the people of Nineveh, complained about this to God, hoping He would change His mind and judge them. Jonah then waited to see what would happen.

Jonah was the only person in the entire story who had no compassion for others. The only compassion he ever showed was toward a plant that benefited him personally. God's love was so profound, on the other hand, that He was concerned not only for the people, but also for the cattle (see Jonah 4:11). How long will we continue to misunderstand God's heart?

Many have been taught wrongly that prophets should eagerly look for judgment, but that is inaccurate. This is not a prophetic trait; it is a *character flaw*. People with little or no compassion delight in judgment. Mature, prophetic people delight in seeing others turning to God and receiving mercy from Him.

ANGRY YOUNG MEN?

In I Kings 13, we find the powerful introduction of a young man of God to the nation of Israel. This man, called as a prophet, exploded onto the scene in a bold and dramatic display of prophetic power, with signs and wonders following his words. His story contains a powerful revelation of God's heart for prophetic ministry.

> Now behold, there came a man of God from Judah to Bethel by the word of the LORD, while Jeroboam was standing by the altar to burn incense.

> And he cried against the altar by the word of the LORD, and said, "O altar, altar, thus says the LORD, 'Behold, a son shall be born to the house of David, Josiah by name; and on you he shall sacrifice the priests of the high places who burn incense on you, and human bones shall be burned on you.'"

> Then he gave a sign the same day, saying, "This is the sign which the LORD has spoken, 'Behold, the altar shall be split apart and the ashes which are on it shall be poured out.'"

> Now it came about when the king heard the saying of the man of God, which he cried against the altar in Bethel, that Jeroboam stretched out his hand from the altar, saying, "Seize him." But his hand which he stretched out against him dried up, so that he could not draw it back to himself.

> The altar also was split apart and the ashes were poured out from the altar, according to the sign which the man of God had given by the word of the LORD (I Kings 13:1-5).

This was dramatic ministry to say the least! God validated His Word with powerful signs. He also verified and protected the young man of God with a curse upon the king. However, a more profound revelation is found in the verbal exchange that follows between the king and the man of God. When the backslidden king asked the young man of God to pray for the restoration of his hand after attempting to kill him, the young man immediately sought the Lord on his behalf.

If he were of the nature many of us believe the Old Covenant prophets to be, he would have said, "How dare you seek God, you backslidden king! Seek your pagan gods, and see if they can heal you. God will not heal you, since you have left Him and have led the people of God astray. From this day until you are gathered to your fathers, you will not lift up nor stretch forth your hand against any man again."

But this was *not* his response. He sought the Lord and the Lord restored the king's hand. Even in this instance, God's purpose was redemptive. God is not possessed by uncontrollable anger, but is merciful and gracious beyond anything we can understand. There are instances when God's judgments will fall, but even then they are redemptive in nature.

This man of God later made a tragic mistake—one which cost him his life. His mistake and the message it contains is much needed for our hour and is addressed in chapter twelve.

MOSES AND THE ROCK

Displaying God as angry when He is not angry is probably one of the more grievous sins we can commit. It is a danger for all called to ministry, but especially those called to speak prophetically. Even Moses succumbed to this error. In Numbers chapter twenty, this was the sin which kept Moses from entering the Promised Land after enduring over thirty-nine years with Israel in the wilderness.

> **And there was no water for the congregation; and they assembled themselves against Moses and Aaron.**

> **The people thus contended with Moses and spoke, saying, "If only we had perished when our brothers perished before the LORD!**

> **"Why then have you brought the LORD's assembly into this wilderness, for us and our beasts to die here?**

> **"And why have you made us come up from Egypt, to bring us in to this wretched place? It is not a place of grain or figs or vines or pomegranates, nor is there water to drink."**

> **Then Moses and Aaron came in from the presence of the assembly to the doorway of the tent of meeting, and fell on their faces. Then the glory of the LORD appeared to them;**

> **and the LORD spoke to Moses, saying,**

> **"Take the rod; and you and your brother Aaron assemble the congregation and speak to the rock before their eyes, that it may yield its water. You shall thus bring forth water for them out of the rock and let the congregation and their beasts drink."**

> **So Moses took the rod from before the LORD, just as He had commanded him;**

and Moses and Aaron gathered the assembly before the rock. And he said to them, "Listen now, you rebels; shall we bring forth water for you out of this rock?"

Then Moses lifted up his hand and struck the rock twice with his rod; and water came forth abundantly, and the congregation and their beasts drank (Numbers 20:2-11).

Can you hear the Lord's tone as He gave Moses the instructions? The Lord instructed him to assemble the people, take his rod and speak to a rock, and it would give forth water. Did God express anger or disgust with His people? Was He frustrated that they doubted Him once again? No. In keeping with the revelation of Himself to Moses, God was gracious, merciful, patient, and long-suffering (see Exodus 34:67).

When Moses began to speak, however, he misrepresented God as being angry at the people for their rebellion. God had expressed no anger, but Moses represented God as angry, impatient, and short-tempered. Moses, provoked and frustrated, struck the rock in anger, instead of speaking to it.

God then issued His judgment against Moses in Numbers 20:12: **"And the Lord said to Moses and Aaron, 'Because you did not believe in (rely on, cling to) Me, to sanctify Me in the eyes of the Israelites, you therefore, shall not bring this congregation into the land which I have given them"** (AMP).

God was not angry with the people, but Moses was, and he communicated his anger as God's anger. Because of this, Moses was unable to lead the people of God into the Promised Land. This was not only a judgment against

Moses; it is a message to us. We can never represent God as capricious in His anger.

Consider how damaging this error was to Israel. Have you ever worked for someone who was easily angered at seemingly insignificant issues? Never knowing what small action or question will set them off, everyone around them is paralyzed by fear, never knowing how their leader will react to any initiative they take. Heed this warning: If we are volatile and communicate that God is also, we will kill the faith and initiative of those we are leading. We cannot lead them into their Promised Land if we present God as volatile and easily angered. He is neither!

JESUS IS THE MODEL

Some current models and teachings about prophetic people excuse this type of anger, but it is clear that God neither endorses or excuses it. We must hold to God's standards regardless of our experience. Prophets are not called and created to be critical, harsh, and angry. These qualities are not inherent in the prophetic gift. If we believe and teach that they are, we will create a new generation of harsh and angry prophets, instead of those who are patient and forgiving like Jesus.

When Jesus' disciples wanted to follow Elijah's model and call down fire from heaven, He instructed them to follow *His* example and life, not Elijah's (see Luke 9:54-56). If we are called to minister prophetically, we are not to model the sin and mistakes of those whose lives are revealed in Scripture. Their lives are laid bare for all to see so that we can avoid and overcome these mistakes. We must honor them for their sacrifices and zeal for God, but we cannot overlook the lessons we must learn from them.

146

OUR EXPERIENCE CAN ROB US

Church leaders must be careful to avoid the mistake outlined by C.S. Lewis in his *Chronicles of Narnia* series. A group of dwarves had been deceived by a counterfeit Aslan, who was the Christ figure of these stories. Deceived by the counterfeit, they determined never to be deceived again. With this posture, they set themselves against the true Aslan when he came, rejecting him and his provision for them. If we are not careful, we can reject the emerging prophetic ministry because of the mistakes and immaturity of those in our past.

I originally said that I disagreed with the pastor's comment about it being dangerous to have the prophetic ministry in a church. His statement is an understandable viewpoint, based on the many spiritual shipwrecks caused by misunderstandings of this ministry. However, it is not dangerous to have the prophetic ministry operative in your congregation—it is dangerous not to have it!

If we do not have the prophetic ministry operative in our midst, we are missing one of two foundational ministries God has given us. What building would stand if half of its foundation was missing? If you are attempting to build without the prophetic ministry as a part of your foundation, you are building something dangerous for habitation.

The prophetic ministry is not to be destructive; by its very nature it is an equipping ministry. The problem has not been the prophetic ministry, but the misunderstandings surrounding it. We cannot throw out the proverbial baby with the bath water. The prophetic, although still a baby in some ways, will eventually mature to be an unprecedented source of strength in the church.

Instead of reacting to the mistakes of the past and allowing these mistakes to define the prophetic ministry, we must endeavor to find God's standards. They are available to us if we choose not to settle for the commonly accepted traditions that currently exist. As we find God's heart and standards and proclaim them, we will begin to see the true spirit of prophecy come forth in those who are emerging in this ministry. They will be a blessing we never could have imagined.

Chapter Nine

WISDOM AND
WARNINGS

As we recover the spirit of prophecy and grow in God's love, there are some practical points we can observe to help us navigate safely in prophetic ministry. This chapter contains practical advice, wisdom, and warnings that can save you, and those you minister to, significant trouble.

This chapter also marks a transition in our training. In previous chapters, encouragement about hearing from God and understanding interpretation and administration have been the focus. At this point, I will now begin balancing that instruction with wisdom and warnings to keep us on the path of life. This chapter and those following speak more specifically to issues encountered by prophetic people.

WISDOM: *Be yourself.*

In any ministry, there is a danger of trying to pattern ourselves after someone who is anointed, successful, or accepted. Because of their past rejections or current insecurities, many prophetically gifted people are especially prone to imitate someone in their ministry style.

We have all encountered people who have been influenced by a prominent minister and have adopted some of their mannerisms. But seldom is this positive. While we are all influenced by those we highly esteem, we must endeavor not to be copies of anyone. Consider the following: A friend of mine was signed to a recording contract when he was only seventeen years old. But his overzealous manager continued to sell my friend to the record company, even after they had signed him. He gushed to the president of the recording label, "You won't believe this kid. He can do a great Ray Charles." To which the man replied, "Yes, but there already *is* a Ray Charles."

Do not fall to imitating others. You can be a good "you," but you will probably be a mediocre someone else. If you act like someone else, people will see it and think you are only acting in your ministry as well. The world needs to experience those who are secure enough in God to be themselves and let God's glory shine through. You must be who God has made you to be.

WARNING: *We know in part, and we prophesy in part.*

Scripture says that we know in part and we prophesy in part (see I Corinthians 13:9). It is imperative not only to realize that we can be wrong, but also to realize that we are seldom completely right. None of us ever really see the whole picture, but only in part. If we possess this humility of heart and mind, we can avoid many unnecessary errors and mistakes.

Remember, regardless of how accurate we may be in our revelation and interpretation, we are only seeing part of the picture. We must realize that there is also more wisdom and insight for a situation than what we are seeing. Be open to receiving additional insight from others and from the Lord.

Some of the most gifted prophetic ministers I know often misinterpret the revelation they receive. God allows this for several reasons: 1) to keep those who are profoundly gifted humble and teachable, 2) to keep us dependent on Him, and, 3) to keep us from wrongly elevating prophetically gifted people to a place of infallibility.

WISDOM: *God often speaks in many different ways at one time.*

When I minister prophetically, I do not receive revelation from the Lord in just one fashion, but several different ways at once. I may receive a simple vision and then recognize some wounds within the person through discerning of spirits at the same time. The discernment I receive dictates how I share the revelation with the person.

Be open to all of the different ways God speaks to you when you are ministering to someone. As we grow in experience, wisdom, and sensitivity, our prophetic ministry can be a powerful tool to set people free.

WARNING: *The spirit of the prophets is subject to the prophets.*

God will seldom have us interrupt a meeting to prophesy. Many people have been taught that when the Holy Spirit reveals something to them, they should immediately interrupt the meeting and prophesy loudly to the congregation. However, this is generally not the best-case scenario.

Our spirit, the motivating influence of our lives, is subject to us (see I Corinthians 14:32). The Holy Spirit will not make us do something through pressuring us. Even though we may feel "an anointing" or "power to prophesy," we still maintain control over our spirits. God does not override our free will to make us do things. We cannot blame God for something that we are doing.

Wisdom: *Practice the word of knowledge.*

Generally, when we begin in the prophetic, we make some mistakes in interpretation. Over the years, I have adopted a simple way to hone my ability to understand how God speaks to me. I practice the word of knowledge. I actually did this much more in earlier years, when my opportunities to minister were limited. Practicing a spiritual gift may sound strange, but it really is not.

I practiced prophecy by silently praying for waiters or bank tellers and then testing what I received by asking them questions. This gave me an opportunity to grow in my understanding and my ability to discern the Lord's voice. Also, many people were ministered to as I practiced. In fact, some were profoundly touched.

Warning: *Do not prophesy beyond your faith.*

Many people have such a passion to function in the higher levels of a word of knowledge that it causes undue trouble. After seeing someone prophesy names, birthdays, and intimate details about a person's life, some novices attempt to prophesy beyond their levels of faith.

Generally, we do not begin at higher levels, but rather progress into more clarity and accuracy as we gain experience and confidence. Jesus often spoke of the kingdom of God in agricultural terms. Likewise, we must recognize that most areas of our spiritual lives progress from the blade to the ear, to the full corn in the ear (see Mark 4:26-28). Do not despise the day of small beginnings (see Zechariah 4:10).

Wisdom: *Stretch beyond your comfort zone.*

While we should not despise the day of small beginnings, we must hunger for more revelation and more accurate interpretations. Generally, God will meet us at our level of hunger. If we feel like we can live without something, we probably will.

One way I stretch beyond my comfort zone when I am ministering is always to ask the Lord for more than what He has given me. If He does and it is a more specific or detailed revelation than what I have been receiving, I test it. I will minister the revelation that I have confidence in and then inform the person that I am not sure about the latter one. Then I will often change from speaking confidently, to asking them if this piece of information is accurate.

If it *is* accurate, then phrasing it as a question generally does not lessen its impact. If it is *not* accurate, or is only partially accurate, we can avoid much misunderstanding by presenting it according to the measure of faith we have (see Romans 12:6).

WARNING: *Do not try to control anyone with prophetic revelation or your reputation.*

Manipulation is bad. Don't do it.

WISDOM: *Honor the written Word.*

The Bible is a wonderful gift from God. When we hide the Word in our hearts, we will grow in all things spiritual, not just the prophetic ministry.

During different seasons, we require all of our prophetic people to present a confirming or justifying Scripture to support what they prophesy. If they have a vision that is not based on biblical symbolism, we require them to also prophesy a Scripture that supports the revelation they have received. This has been a fruitful discipline for our teams.

WARNING: *Listen to your pastor.*

Your pastors generally will not see what you see prophetically. Remember, they are pastors, *not* prophetic ministers. Honor them, even if they do not understand your revelation at times. You need them as much as they need you and possibly more. If you want to mature spiritually, you must respect and honor your pastors.

WISDOM: *Follow the presence of the Lord.*

Many times when we are seeking an interpretation, we need to look for God's presence as much as we look for understanding. Often, when we get off course in our pursuit of an interpretation, we will sense confusion in our souls. This is God's way of saying, "Don't look here." God often leads us by His presence or the absence of it.

WARNING: *Serve with your gift, but do not seek to establish yourself or your authority with it.*

It is important to step out in ministry and serve others with the revelation God gives us. However, trying to rule with our prophetic gift is another matter. We must never seek to draw people to ourselves with revelation or prophecy.

Spiritual authority is given to us in God's timing. We cannot try to elevate ourselves to positions of authority. Instead, we choose the place of a servant and give ourselves to helping others. When we have learned to serve God by serving others, we have already learned leadership.

WISDOM: *Find mature prophetic people to disciple you.*

We can learn the lessons others have learned throughout their lifetimes, if we will seek out their friendship and wisdom. They can help us avoid the mistakes they have already made.

WARNING: *Prophesy what the Lord shows you and nothing else.*

Many prophetic people have difficulty starting and stopping when the Lord does. Here is a good rule of thumb: When the Lord shows you something, tell the person. When He stops showing you things, stop talking. **"When words are many, sin is not absent, but he who holds his tongue is wise" (Proverbs 10:19 NIV).** Be wise. Keep your prophetic words concise.

WISDOM: *Smile when you prophesy.*

People often pay more attention to our faces than to what we are saying. It is possible to frighten people with our faces while we are trying to encourage them with our words. Be encouraging with your face and body language. Minister the love of God with every opportunity and in every way possible.

As I stated before, if I am standing and begin ministering prophetically to someone who is seated, I will kneel down so that I am not towering over them. I would rather minister to someone from a position beneath them than above them. Many people are automatically intimidated by the concept of prophecy, so I try to literally position myself as a servant (beneath them) while ministering.

WARNING: *Do not try to be the Holy Spirit to anyone.*

We are called to encourage, not to push or force anyone to obey God. New Testament prophecy by believers is generally not the confrontational style we have seen or imagined. Prophecy for the average believer is meant to build, encourage, and comfort, not rebuke and chasten.

WISDOM: *Ask permission before laying hands on someone.*

We do not have a God-given right to lay hands on any person, and we should ask God for permission before doing so. If we do not get a check in our spirit, we are then clear to move forward and ask the person if we have their permission to lay hands on them.

Having a prophetic revelation for someone does not allow us to violate their personal sovereignty. They have the right to determine who and when someone lays hands on them for ministry, and we should never assume that we have this right.

WARNING: *Get healed. Your "discernment" may really be fear and suspicion.*

We have to get over the wounds and rejection of the past and now is a good time. When we are wounded, we will react in our soul and misinterpret what we feel from God. Many people receive negative words about the leadership of their congregation because of past wounds from other leaders.

James 3:17 says that **"the wisdom that is from above is first pure, then peaceable, gentle, and easy to be entreated, full of mercy and good fruits..."** (KJV). If we are wounded in our souls, our discernment is suspect. We must be healed of the past to accurately see prophetically.

WISDOM: *Walk away when you are angry.*

Misrepresenting God as angry when He was not disqualified Moses from leading Israel into their Promised

Land (see Numbers 20:12). Whenever we become tired or provoked, we must keep our mouths closed. Moses was provoked in his spirit and spoke unadvisedly in anger (see Psalm 106:33). It is better to excuse ourselves when we feel angry or frustrated. If we prophesy in anger, we will curse rather than bless others, and we will bring judgment on ourselves.

WARNING: *Avoid prophesying "second heaven" revelations.*

Many times prophetic revelation will take the form of us receiving a vision or dream of someone participating in sin. This type of revelation would seem to contradict the idea that prophecy is for encouragement, edification, and comfort. But these types of revelation really fit within that context if we consider that in the majority of these cases, the Lord is revealing to us what the enemy has planned and not what is currently happening. What is being shown to us is the plan of the enemy, not the purpose of God. We must also realize that what we are seeing is probably not the person's plan. We should not automatically assume that the person is desiring to walk in this sin, but rather that the enemy is laying a trap for them.

Paul said in I Corinthians 13:7 that love hopes all things and believes all things. In all ministry, we should start from the position of hoping and believing that people want to do the right thing. Most Christians are trying with everything they have to serve God and live righteously. We can injure people if we assume their intentions are bad and accuse them accordingly.

God will often allow us to see the plan of the enemy. Some people who do not understand God's heart or purpose in giving revelation will often interpret the plan of the enemy as the purpose of God.

We cannot prophesy this kind of revelation to someone as being the plan of God. The Lord will show us the enemy's plan so that we can nullify it, not help it come to pass by prophesying it. One of Satan's greatest tactics is to communicate his lie as God's truth. We must be discerning and know God's heart and plan.

Wisdom: *Do not pray the prophetic word; speak it.*

Some people try to avoid the accountability involved in directly speaking a prophetic word. They feel that if they pray the word over someone, the person will know it is prophetic and they (the person prophesying) will not have to deal with potentially giving a wrong word.

This is not a good idea for two reasons. First, we must always walk in faith and we should also be as forthright as possible. Changing the way we minister to accommodate our fear allows the enemy continued access in our lives. Fear is sin and should be repented of, not accommodated. Second, we should be clear with people and not leave them to wonder whether or not we are speaking prophetically. They need to judge prophecy, and to do so, they need to know when we are prophesying and when we are simply praying for them.

Note: Some ministries have trained their people to minister this way in renewal-type meetings and I support the reasoning behind this. The Lord's purpose in renewal-type meetings is often for the person to be ministered to through His presence rather than through words of encouragement. Ministering prophetically in this setting can interrupt the purpose of the Lord by causing the person to disengage from the Lord to listen to us speak.

In conclusion, one good discipline for prophetic people is to read I Corinthians 13 every day for the rest of our lives. Walking in the love of God will enable us to avoid most of the mistakes that have been commonly made by immature prophetic people. As we pursue love, let us grow in wisdom and heed these warnings. Our prophetic ministry will become more beneficial in building the church as we avoid these mistakes.

Chapter Ten

THE ORIGIN OF FALSE PROPHETS

Aside from wisdom and warnings, we need to avoid certain pitfalls and see the danger of wrong motivations. So far, I have focused primarily on helping to release people into the prophetic gifts by explaining the principles of receiving, interpreting, and administrating prophetic words. Now that we have established God's purpose, ways, and means concerning prophetic gifts, we must discuss the issue of false prophets.

When we speak of false prophets in this book, we are not talking about astrologers, psychics, and fortune-tellers. Although these are clearly false, I doubt that anyone reading this book is in danger of replicating these errors. Rather, false prophets in the church are those who are destructive, ministering with a true prophetic gift, but without prophetic character. The fruit of false prophets is division, strife, and discord in the congregations they touch.

We must understand the origins of a false prophet for three basic reasons. First, if we understand their origins and motivations, we can more easily discern the false prophets who come into our congregations to scatter the flock. Second, this understanding will enable us to help young, emerging prophetic ministries avoid these pitfalls as they mature. Third, if we are called to the prophetic ministry, we must understand the traps laid by the enemy to ensnare us.

The Spirit of Prophecy

Being called to ministry means that we are called to represent the Lord. We represent Him in two primary ways—with our words and with our lives. Revelation 19:10 says that **"the testimony of Jesus is the spirit of prophecy."** We must not live our lives or use our words carelessly if we are to accurately represent Jesus, the faithful and true Witness (see Revelation 3:14).

The Lord gave me a dream years ago to help me understand the power of my words. In the dream, I was standing with a group of friends on the construction site of a new home. Building materials and construction tools were lying on the ground around this unfinished house. All at once, different people began throwing steel rods, shovels, and other building tools at me. I easily swatted these aside without any of them harming me. Finally, out of frustration at people throwing dangerous objects at me, I picked up a small screwdriver and gently tossed it at someone. The screwdriver sailed across the landscape and sank deeply into my friend's belly. He doubled over as blood began flowing out of his stomach. I was panic stricken when I realized what I had done. The dream ended.

The construction site represented the church, which is being built into the Lord's house. The people on the construction site represented members of the body of Christ. The different objects being thrown by individuals were their words. Although heavy, pointed words were thrown at me, I could easily cast them aside.

However, my words, no matter how small and softly "thrown," would go deep into the belly (spirits) of others. Although this was a specific message and warning to me, it is also a general message for all who are called prophetically.

Our words contain spiritual power and authority. We must not throw them around carelessly. While other peoples' words may not hurt us, we can kill with ours because of the power God has put behind them.

Ministers who witness of Jesus verbally should also witness of Him with their lives. John 1:14 declares that **"the Word became flesh."** Just as Jesus was the Word made flesh, so the Word of God should also be made flesh in us. It must not only be our message; we must also live it. While this is true of all ministries, it is especially true of the prophetic because we are speaking for God.

Because of the dramatic demonstrations of power and revelation that often accompany this ministry, it is especially important that any weakness of character be openly and honestly dealt with. A wise man once stated that power corrupts, and absolute power corrupts absolutely. Although not an immutable spiritual truth, it will be true in the case of those who are called to walk in God's power if certain wrong motivations are not dealt with by God.

THE PROGRESSION OF FALSE PROPHETS

While we all fall short in numerous areas, there are three basic character flaws from which those called to prophetic ministry must be delivered in order to stay on the path of life and true ministry. Each of these flaws involve selfishness and are found in the epistle of Jude. Jude's letter to the church was written primarily as a warning about those who are false prophets and the believer's response to them. In one of the most dramatic and fear inspiring encounters I have ever had with the Lord, He spoke the following verse to me in 1988 to explain the characteristics of a false prophet.

Woe unto them! For they have gone in the way of Cain, and ran greedily after the error of Balaam for reward, and perished in the gainsaying of Korah (Jude 11 KJV).

Cain, Balaam, and Korah each represent a different character flaw that will pervert our ministries if we do not recognize them at work in us and then quickly repent. They not only represent a different flaw, but also a progression of selfishness that will cause us to become false in our ministry.

CAIN

Cain represents those who are plagued with the character flaw of self-will. The name "Cain" means *maker* or *fabricator* or *one who makes his own way*. Self-will is the desire to do things our own way, instead of God's way or the way of those whom He has placed as authorities in our lives. Cain's attempt to fulfill God's plan according to his own methods (see Genesis 4) is a classic example of self-will and its results. When Cain's offering was rejected, he reacted badly. Instead of acknowledging that his way was wrong and that God's way was right, he became angry and depressed. Even after God Himself confronted Cain, he still did not turn from his own way. His depression and anger gave place to a spirit of murder as he killed his own brother.

Our self-will possesses the power to pervert our perspective in the same way. If we launch prematurely into prophetic ministry through our self-will and are not accepted in that ministry, we will become depressed and angry, eventually spiritually and emotionally destroying those around us.

Many false prophets have devastated entire congregations by using their revelation gifts in self-will to attack the church's leaders. Even after leaving a trail of division and strife wherever they go, many of these will not listen to correction. At this point self-will, anger, and depression combine to form self-pity, which is possibly the greatest detriment to spiritual growth and maturity that exists.

Self-pity is an enemy of our souls that keeps us making excuses and placing the blame on others so as to avoid taking the responsibility that could help cure us. Those who are going in the way of Cain are self-willed to the point of being unteachable by anyone, including God!

Self-will is the root of much sin. We see this first with Lucifer and then Adam. Each sinned by choosing his own way over God's. As they did, each released evil throughout the world in unprecedented ways. We are deceiving ourselves if we think that our choices affect only us. If we have been given a place of responsibility and authority with God's children, any fall that we experience will injure those under our care. If self-will remains a part of our character, we will eventually be captain to devastating spiritual shipwrecks.

There is often much rejection for those who are called prophetically. This is true for many reasons, including the supernatural, and often strange phenomenon surrounding this ministry. However, one reason many prophetic ministers experience rejection is God's response to the sin of self-will. As Lucifer acted in self-will, he was cast out of heaven (see Isaiah 14:12-15). As Adam acted in self-will, he was cast out of the Garden (see Genesis 3:23-24). As Cain acted in self-will and then murdered his brother, God declared that he would be a fugitive and a vagabond throughout the earth (see Genesis 4:11-12).

Jude 13 describes false prophets as **"wandering stars."** This is characteristic of those who are false in ministry; they wander from one place to another without any set course. The rejection that arises from self-will has caused them to deviate from the path which God has set for their lives. If we are wise, we will cease from this sin the moment we are convicted of it. If we do, we can find a place of acceptance in life and fruitfulness in ministry. If we do not, we will soon progress from the way of Cain to the error of Balaam.

BALAAM

Balaam's name means *devourer of the people* or *conqueror of the people*. He represents those who devour the sheep or use the people for their own gain. The Bible says that Balaam was once a prophet to whom God Himself came (see Numbers 22:9). However, when tempted to use his prophetic gift to obtain riches and glory for himself at the expense of God's people, he eventually gave in.

This may be the greatest temptation to those in leadership. Will we use our position, power, and authority to serve the people or ourselves? Jude, describing this characteristic of false prophets, said that they were **"feeding themselves without fear" (see Jude 12 KJV)**, disregarding the needs of the people, and **"walking after their own lusts" (see Jude 16 KJV)**.

There are three basic arenas for this temptation—financial or political, emotional, and sexual. Financial and political gain was the first area in which Balaam was tempted. Balak, king of Moab, offered him great riches and authority if only he would use his prophetic gift for Balak's purposes. Most today will never be confronted with anything so blatant, but are we tempted to subtly change the message God has given us in order to make it more acceptable to people who promise to provide us with finances or influence? Proverbs 15:27 states, **"He who profits illicitly troubles his own house; but he who hates bribes will live."** We would do well to heed this warning.

It is proper that those who preach the gospel should derive their living from the ministry (see I Corinthians 9:14). But if we begin catering our ministry to those who have wealth and influence, instead of faithfully ministering to everyone whom God has put in our charge, we are nothing more than spiritual harlots selling ourselves for temporal rewards. If, like Balaam, we are respecters of men, we may remain true for a while. However, when the more honorable princes come, we will give in to this temptation and go with them, believing that God has sent us (see Numbers 22:20-22).

Possibly the most subtle and therefore dangerous aspect of this character flaw is the temptation to devour the glory and esteem that comes from the people. If we are nourished by the acclaim people attempt to heap on us, we will soon be ministering for the sake of that recognition. We will again be tempted to change the message so that it pleases the people. Consider Jesus' words to the religious professionals of His day:

"He who speaks from himself seeks his own glory; but He who is seeking the glory of the One who sent Him, He is true, and there is no unrighteousness in Him" (John 7:18).

"How can ye believe, which receive honor one of another, and seek not the honor that cometh from God only?" (John 5:44 KJV)

These were looking for their glory from one another. Are we inclined to do the same? Are we tempted to speak words that will bring about our own glory? If we are seeking to find our personal significance in those to whom we minister, our ministry will be greatly perverted. We then become more concerned with the opinions of the people than with the opinions of God. The tendency to receive and begin craving the glory of the people is often intricately linked to the rejection that many have experienced. Regardless, the Scriptures are clear: If we are still seeking to please men, we cannot truly be the bondservants of Christ (see Galatians 1:10).

Another aspect of this Balaam character flaw, which often comes through the doorway of rejection is sexual immorality. Some, who have not been healed of their rejection, have fallen to looking for acceptance in illicit relationships with those to whom they are ministering. Because of the dramatic and supernatural nature of prophetic ministry, there is a tendency to be awed not only by the gift, but by the possessor of it. Some prophetic ministers, still harboring deep rejection, have used this as a means to develop inappropriate emotional relationships. From that point, the fall into sexual immorality can happen quickly.

To avoid the error of Balaam, it is imperative to remember that our true inheritance is in heaven. As Proverbs 20:21 states, **"An inheritance hastily gotten [by greedy, unjust means] at the beginning, in the end will not be blessed"** (AMP). Balaam, a prophet to whom the Lord Himself once came, died as a soothsayer (see Joshua 13:22). If we are not willing to wait for our rewards in heaven, we also can digress from prophets to diviners whose end is not blessed.

Korah

Korah literally means *bald* or *uncovered*. He represents the rebellion often present in the lives and ministry of false prophets. In Numbers 16, we find the scenario that defines Korah and his gainsaying.

Korah and other men of renown in Israel rose up against Moses and Aaron with the accusation that they had taken too much authority upon themselves, since all of Israel was holy in God's eyes. This seemingly democratic move was actually inspired by Korah's own desire for more authority. Likewise, many false prophets today will try to use a doctrine of equality as a means of establishing themselves in authority.

The fact that Korah was a man of renown and fame in Israel had no bearing on the amount of spiritual authority he possessed. God, not the people, had placed Moses and Aaron in authority. In like manner today, true spiritual authority does not come from the church—it comes from God! It is possible that Korah was called by God to a greater position of leadership in the nation of Israel than he currently possessed, but he did not endure the test of patience.

There is a process by which we all enter into the ministry that God has for us. In general, this process is designed to deal with the character issues that would ultimately destroy us and the people to whom we minister. The final test for most of us is the test of patience. Just as with Jesus, the enemy will offer us a crown without a cross. But like the Son of God, we must be willing to accept only the path dictated by the Father, and it is a more narrow path. If we are impatient and anxious to be in authority, then we are still unfit for that authority.

Learning to wait upon God is an acknowledgment that we understand the source of true spiritual authority. True spiritual authority does not depend on us or our giftedness; it depends on God's choice. It is possible that Korah possessed greater gifts and abilities than Moses, but he was not God's leadership choice at that time. We do not fulfill our ministry through our own strength and abilities, but through God's anointing, which He places upon those whom He chooses.

When Korah stood against him, Moses replied that God would show whom He had chosen. If we are seeking our own advancement instead of the establishment of God's kingdom, then we also will disregard God's choice. When we reject God's choice, we are really rejecting God. Unless the self-will of Cain and the self-seeking of Balaam in our lives is dealt with, they will evolve into a rebellion that rejects God's anointed leadership, and even God Himself!

This same gainsaying is the source of the gossip and accusation pervading the church today. It is fueled by the selfish ambition of those who are gifted but impatient. Jude, describing this characteristic of false prophets writes, **"These are grumblers, finding fault ... they speak arrogantly, flattering people for the sake of gaining an advantage" (Jude 16).**

Our choices are clear: We can serve those whom God has chosen for our leaders, or we can cultivate the hearts of the people toward ourselves in order to gain illegal and untimely spiritual authority. This type of political maneuvering is typical of those who have become false in ministry. Self-will in Cain becomes self-seeking in Balaam, and eventually self-exaltation in Korah. Jesus said that **"whoever exalts himself shall be humbled"** (see **Matthew 23:12**). Consider the judgment of Korah and his accomplices.

And the earth opened her mouth, and swallowed them up, and their houses, and all the men that appertained unto Korah, and all their goods.

They, and all that appertained to them, went down alive into the pit, and the earth closed upon them: and they perished from among the congregation (Numbers 16:32-33 KJV).

Korah and his cronies were raptured to hell. They literally went into the pit alive! Korah's judgment is a prophetic warning. When rebellion of this order has set into the life of those prophetically called, they enter into the dominion of hell and become false prophets. At this point, they have crossed a line and catastrophic judgment is imminent. However, this judgment can be redemptive even at this late stage if they will acknowledge their sin, repent, and submit to God's process of restoration.

GIFTS AND FRUIT

We must come into a better understanding about the prophetic ministry. One dangerous tendency has been for the church to accept so open-mindedly anything that calls itself prophetic that when we bend over our brains fall out! It is proper to honor and esteem those who are gifted, but we must never allow their giftedness to overshadow their character. Jesus Himself said that we should judge men by their fruit and not solely by their gifts.

Beware of false prophets, which come to you in sheep's clothing, but inwardly they are ravening wolves.

Ye shall know them by their fruits... (Matthew 7:15-16 KJV).

171

Some in ministry today have left the relationship with the Lord that they once possessed. They have departed from the path of life, yet they continue to minister in the supernatural gifts given to them by God. Romans 11:29 says that **"the gifts and calling of God are without repentance" (KJV)**. God does not take away the spiritual gifts He gives to us. Therefore, we must know the manner of life of those who labor among us (see I Thessalonians 5:12).

How Should We Then Live?

This may be hard to comprehend, but most false prophets are still true Christians. Again, we are not discussing those who are obviously false, such as astrologers and psychics, but rather those who have fallen to the errors we have discussed. Many who are truly called of God have become false because they presumed to walk in a ministry to which they were not called, or because they did so prematurely. By making one of these errors, they stepped outside of the Lord's plan into their own and have been taken captive by the enemy.

However, they are still heirs of salvation. The greatest victory is to see these restored to the Lord's desire for their lives. They need to turn from their selfish motivations to a loving and forgiving God. Because it is God's desire for all to be saved, we must always keep salvation, redemption, and restoration foremost in our interaction with everyone.

Consider Jude's instruction for our response to these false prophets:

> **Keep yourselves in the love of God, looking for the mercy of our Lord Jesus Christ unto eternal life.**
>
> **And of some have compassion, making a difference.**

And others save with fear, pulling them out of the fire; hating even the garment spotted by the flesh (Jude 21-23 KJV).

We are now under a better covenant with better promises than were Cain, Balaam, and Korah. One promise is that God chastens and disciplines those whom He loves (see Hebrews 12:5-8). If God brings discipline to those who have become false in ministry and they submit to it, God is well able to change them. Indeed, He is able to change any person who submits to Him without excuses.

If you are overtaken in any of these areas, turn to God and to those who can help you overcome your sin and character flaws. Quit making excuses for yourself and obtain the character of Christ. There is still time to change the course that you are on. Like Jezebel who called herself a prophetess but was false, God is giving you space to repent (see Revelation 2:20-29).

If you are a pastor, help the emerging prophetic ministers in your congregation. Be loving *and* firm with them. Scripture declares that **"open rebuke is better than secret love" (Proverbs 27:5 KJV)**. Hold their feet to the fire. If they get burned, you can help to heal them. You are called to watch over their souls and speak into their lives, and you will give an account to God for your oversight (see Hebrews 13:17). If false prophets come into your fold, you should try to help them, but not at the expense of sacrificing the sheep.

CONCLUSION

My experience has shown me several potential dangers in presenting these truths. First, those who need a word like this are prone to not receive it. Therefore, if you are called to prophetic ministry, ask God to examine you and see if there is any hurtful way in you. Also submit yourself to those to whom you are accountable for their input. If you do not have such relationships, you need to ask the Lord to help you find them quickly.

The second danger is that many who do not need this message will receive it because of their humility. These will have a tendency to stop ministering until their motives are 100 percent pure. Hear this word: God does not want you to stop ministering; He wants you to minister in power and with His character. Continue in the way of the Lord while receiving the correction He brings to you.

Third, many immature prophets look like false prophets. Therefore, if some leaders overreact to this message, there is a danger of destroying in their infancy many who are currently being groomed by God for prophetic ministry. Pastors, instead of erring in this way, learn to recognize the young prophets in your midst and help guide them into God's perfect will for their lives.

Regardless of these and other reactions, we must address these issues and press forward. God is restoring the prophetic ministry to the church and we must receive it. We must understand these wrong motivations in order to not only discern the false, but to also receive and pastor the emerging prophetic ministry so that it comes to fullness in our midst.

Chapter Eleven

THE ROOT OF DECEPTION

Accompanying the problems arising from the wrong motives discussed in the previous chapter is the issue of idolatry. Whenever we "hear from God," it is usually subjective in nature to some degree. Seldom is it completely objective. Rather, we hear God speaking through the issues that exist in our hearts or our minds. As such, it is extremely important to have clean hearts and pure minds, since impurity can taint what we hear from God.

Because the life of Balaam provides amazing insight into the terrible dangers of deception accompanying idolatry, his example also trumpets a stern warning of how even someone who is gifted prophetically can become deceived in their guidance from God.

Two significant benefits can be gained from understanding Balaam's life. First, there are practical guidelines on following God's leading. Second, we see that the degree to which we have allowed idolatry to remain in our hearts is the degree to which we are susceptible to deception and delusion. Seen correctly, this awareness can help us choose the Lord's fear instead of presumption.

The Israelites journeyed and encamped in the plains of Moab, on the east side of the Jordan [River] at Jericho.

And Balak [the king of Moab] son of Zippor saw all that Israel had done to the Amorites.

And Moab was terrified at the people *and* full of dread, because they were many; Moab was distressed *and* overcome with fear because of the Israelites.

And Moab said to the elders of Midian, Now will this multitude lick up all that is round about us, as the ox licks up the grass of the field. So Balak son of Zippor the king of the Moabites at that time,

Sent messengers to Balaam [a foreteller of events] son of Beor at Pethor, which is by the [Euphrates] River, even to the land of the children of his people, to say to him, There is a people come out from Egypt; behold, they cover the face of the earth, and they have settled down *and* dwell opposite me.

Now come, I beg of you, curse this people for me, for they are too powerful for me. Perhaps I may be able to defeat them and drive them out of the land, for I know that he whom you bless is blessed, and he whom you curse is cursed.

And the elders of Moab and of Midian departed with the rewards of foretelling in their hand, and they came to Balaam and told him the words of Balak.

And he said to them, Lodge here tonight and I will bring you word as the Lord may speak to me. And the princes of Moab abode with Balaam [that night].

And God came to Balaam, and said, What men are these with you?

And Balaam said to God, Balak son of Zippor, king of Moab, has sent to me, saying,

Behold, the people who came out of Egypt cover the face of the earth; come now, curse them for me. Perhaps I shall be able to fight against them and drive them out.

And God said to Balaam, You shall not go with them; you shall not curse the people, for they are blessed.

And Balaam rose up in the morning, and said to the princes of Balak, Go back to your own land, for the Lord refuses to permit me to go with you.

So the princes of Moab rose up and went to Balak, and said, Balaam refuses to come with us.

Then Balak again sent princes, more of them and more honorable than the first ones.

And they came to Balaam, and said to him, Thus says Balak son of Zippor, I beg of you, let nothing hinder you from coming to me.

For I will promote you to very great honor, and I will do whatever you tell me; so come, I beg of you, curse this people for me.

And Balaam answered the servants of Balak, If Balak would give me his house full of silver and gold, I cannot go beyond the word of the Lord my God, to do less or more.

Now therefore, I pray you, tarry here again tonight that I may know what more the Lord will say to me.

And God came to Balaam at night, and said to him, If the men come to call you, rise up and go with them, but still only what I tell you may you do.

And Balaam rose up in the morning and saddled his donkey and went with the princes of Moab.

And God's anger was kindled because he went, and the Angel of the Lord stood in the way as an adversary against him. Now he was riding upon his donkey, and his two servants were with him.

And the donkey saw the Angel of the Lord standing in the way and His sword drawn in His hand, and the donkey turned aside out of the way and went into the field. And Balaam struck the donkey to turn her into the way (**Numbers 22:1-23 AMP**).

Consider Balaam's strengths. His first mention in Scripture shows God appearing and speaking to him (verse 9). Additionally, Balaam's prophetic ability must have been astounding since Balak considered Balaam's gift to be his only hope of victory over Israel (verse 6). As a foundation for our examination of his life, it is apparent that Balaam heard from God and that God hearkened to his words spoken prophetically.

GETTING WHAT YOU WANT

The first question to examine is why would God want to kill someone who obeys His Word? In verse 20, God told Balaam to go with the princes of Moab, but to speak only what He told him. Then in verse 22, God sent an angel to kill Balaam for obeying Him! How can God want to kill someone for obeying His word?

Upon closer inspection, it appears that God never intended for Balaam to go to Balak. His original instruction was concise and clear, prohibiting Balaam from going (verse 12). Later, when more honorable princes came offering limitless rewards, Balaam, motivated by his lust for wealth, inquired if God had changed His mind. This time God instructed Balaam to go (verse 20), became angry when he went, and then released an angel to kill him for going! (verse 22)

Our second question is why would God give Balaam permission to go to Balak the second time instead of simply forbidding him again from going? The third question is how can someone hear God as clearly as Balaam and still walk in such profound deception? Both of these answers are found in God's way of dealing with those who have set up idols in their hearts. God revealed this dealing to Ezekiel.

Then came certain of the elders of Israel to me, and sat before me.

And the word of the Lord came to me:

Son of man, these men have set up their idols in their hearts and put the stumbling block of their iniquity *and* guilt before their faces; should I permit Myself to be inquired of at all by them?

Therefore speak to them, and say to them, Thus says the Lord God: Every man of the house of Israel who takes his idols [of self-will and unsubmissiveness] into his heart and puts

the stumbling block of his iniquity [idols of silver and gold] before his face, and yet comes to the prophet [to inquire of him], I the Lord will answer him, answer him according to the multitude of his idols;

That I may lay hold of the house of Israel in the thoughts of their own mind *and* heart, because they are all estranged from Me through their idols (Ezekiel 14:1-5 AMP).

God will speak to us through our idols. If we set up idols in our hearts, harboring a desire for something contrary to God's revealed will and then inquire of God concerning His will, He will speak in agreement with our idols. By inquiring of God concerning something we know to be contrary to His revealed will, we are already participating in deception. If we know His will, we do not need to ask—we just need to obey!

Balaam knew God's will in this situation. It was revealed in God's first word to him. Just as God spoke through the idols of desire for wealth and prominence that Balaam had allowed to take root in his heart, so He will speak to us through our idols as well. If we need a practical reason to choose the fear of God, here it is: God will participate in our deception, if we continue in it.

DECEIVED BY DECEPTION

One of the main problems with deception is that we are not aware we are deceived. In fact, the most deceived people generally believe themselves to be following the Lord's own voice. Consider the rest of Balaam's story:

And the donkey saw the Angel of the Lord standing in the way and His sword drawn in

His hand, and the donkey turned aside out of the way, and went into the field. And Balaam struck the donkey to turn her into the way.

But the Angel of the Lord stood in a path of the vineyards, a wall on this side and a wall on that side.

And when the donkey saw the Angel of the Lord, she thrust herself against the wall and crushed Balaam's foot against it, and he struck her again.

And the Angel of the Lord went further and stood in a narrow place where there was no room to turn either to the right hand or to the left.

And when the donkey saw the Angel of the Lord, she fell down under Balaam, and Balaam's anger was kindled and he struck the donkey with his staff.

And the Lord opened the mouth of the donkey, and she said to Balaam, What have I done to you that you should strike me these three times?

And Balaam said to the donkey, Because you have ridiculed *and* provoked me! I wish there were a sword in my hand, for now I would kill you!

And the donkey said to Balaam, Am not I your donkey, upon which you have ridden all your life long until this day? Was I ever accustomed to do so to you? And he said, No.

Then the Lord opened Balaam's eyes, and he saw the Angel of the Lord standing in the way with His sword drawn in His hand; and he bowed his head, and fell on his face.

And the Angel of the Lord said to him, Why have you struck your donkey these three times? See, I came out to stand against *and* resist you, for your behavior is willfully obstinate *and* contrary before Me.

And the ass saw Me and turned from Me these three times. If she had not turned from Me, surely I would have slain you, and saved her alive.

Balaam said to the Angel of the Lord, I have sinned, for I did not know You stood in the way against me. But now, if my going displeases You, I will return.

The Angel of the Lord said to Balaam, Go with the men, but you shall speak only what I tell you. So Balaam went with the princes of Balak (Numbers 22:23-35 AMP).

Although Balaam was prophetically gifted, consider how spiritually dull he had become through his idolatry. Not only did Balaam not see the angel sent to kill him, but when his donkey began talking to him, Balaam talked back! Apparently he never realized how miraculous this was because he was so focused on the wealth and honor waiting for him. If a donkey began questioning *you* on something, wouldn't you be more prone to question how and why he was talking rather than argue with him?

Even after seeing the angel armed with a sword, Balaam did not acknowledge his sin in going to Moab against God's will. Although it may appear that he repented in verse 34, a closer examination reveals that he only answered the angel's question from verse 32 about wrongly beating his donkey, accepting responsibility for that.

Unbelievably, Balaam continued pressing forward to Moab. He told the angel he would go back home *if* his going to Balak was displeasing to God. *If* it was displeasing? God sending an angel to kill him more than implied it was displeasing! Balaam, driven by the idols of prominence and wealth, was blinded to God's will. Remarkably, he continued to ask God's permission to go. Even more remarkably, the Lord once again answered Balaam through the idols in his heart, instructing him to go.

LEARN THE LESSONS

Balaam is not the only example we have of this phenomenon. Recent church history resounds with the tragedies of those who, after years of faithful service, have died in disrepute by following the idols of their hearts, believing their actions to be God's will. If we are wise, we will learn our lessons from the lives of others. Several practical insights are found in Balaam's life, as well as a general warning about the danger of idolatry.

1)   Go with God's revealed will.

God's will is revealed primarily in His written Word, and we should never go against it. Any leading from God that contradicts Scripture must be judged as inaccurate. In Balaam's case, he did not have the written Word, he only had God's revealed will from previous encounters. But God's first message was definitive and conclusive. There was no room for Balaam to wonder about God's intentions. However, motivated by his lust for riches and honor, he chose to ignore God's revealed will and entered into deception by seeking another word.

2) God seldom changes His mind.

Balaam wanted to hear that God had changed His mind, so God obliged him. As He explained to Ezekiel, God spoke in accordance with the idols set up in Balaam's heart. This is an important lesson for us. As the authority structures in our society have become more lenient, many have been deceived into believing that God has also become lenient, changing His will to accommodate our wishes. However, if motivated by our idols we continue to ask concerning His will, we may receive permission, but only at a great cost spiritually.

3) We must carefully judge any "word" from God that contradicts an earlier word, especially if our motives are suspect.

Even though He spoke in accordance with Balaam's idols, God still provided an angelic witness that going to Balak was against His revealed will. God says to Balaam in verse 20, **"If the men come to call thee, rise up, and go with them" (KJV).** This should have been an obvious indication to Balaam that what he was hearing was tainted by his own desires. The men were already there! Did God not know that they had already come to call Balaam to go with them? By this obvious discrepancy, Balaam should have realized that he was hearing a word contaminated by his own desires. Likewise, we must judge carefully any leading that we "hear" from the Lord which has questionable content.

4) Once we enter into deception it is difficult to get free.

After an encounter with the angel sent to kill him, Balaam still did not forfeit his idols. He was so consumed by the lust for riches and honor that he asked the angel, "If it is displeasing to you, I will turn back." *If* it was displeasing? It was displeasing enough that the angel was going to cut his head off! How much more displeasing could it get?

Instead of acknowledging that he was acting contrary to God's will and turning to go back home, Balaam continues on his journey to Moab. God's Word filtered through the idols of Balaam's heart comes forth as, **"Go with the men, but you shall speak only the word which I shall tell you" (verse 35)**. This was the same Word that he obeyed, which almost got him killed.

This is a severe warning to us. If we willfully choose to believe a lie, God will allow us to believe it. Self-will can lead to destruction.

5) *We must possess the fear of the Lord in order to stay free from idolatry and deception.*

"The fear of the LORD is the beginning of wisdom..." (Proverbs 9:10 KJV). If we do not have the fear of God, we do not really have His wisdom. Without the fear of God, we will probably only have a wisdom that is earthly or demonic and produces confusion (see James 3:14-17). On the contrary, having the fear of God will cause us to depart from evil. **"By mercy and truth iniquity is purged: and by the fear of the LORD men depart from evil" (Proverbs 16:6 KJV).**

GETTING OUT OF IDOLATRY

We must deal radically and ruthlessly with any idol or wrong desire that God reveals in our lives. Jesus not only gave us a mandate for dealing with our hands (representing our actions), but also for dealing with our eyes (representing our thoughts).

"You have heard that it was said, 'You shall not commit adultery';

"but I say to you, that everyone who looks on a woman to lust for her has committed adultery with her already in his heart.

"And if your right eye makes you stumble, tear it out, and throw it from you; for it is better for you that one of the parts of your body perish, than for your whole body to be thrown into hell.

"And if your right hand makes you stumble, cut it off, and throw it from you; for it is better for you that one of the parts of your body perish, than for your whole body to go into hell" (Matthew 5:27-30).

God will not overlook our lust, and we must not condone it either. Idolatrous thoughts are not only dangerous—they are deadly.

> Then when lust has conceived, it gives birth to sin; and when sin is accomplished, it brings forth death.
>
> Do not be deceived, my beloved brethren (James 1:15-16).

We are living in wonderful, but perilous times. We have great reason to rejoice for all God is doing and will do, but we cannot presumptuously allow idolatry to remain in our lives. Do not be deceived: we will eventually do whatever is in our hearts, whether it is God's will or our own, which is idolatry.

We must not only pursue the Lord with all our heart, soul, mind, and strength, but we must also cast away any idol that is revealed in our hearts. We cannot play with sin or sinful thoughts. God is our Father and wants to protect us, but we must not disregard His correction or the warnings from the lives of those who have gone before us. Do not allow yourself to be deceived by deception.

Chapter Twelve

OVERCOMING REJECTION

One of the main problems to be overcome by many emerging prophetic ministries is the stronghold of rejection. Rejection is a byproduct of Christianity, but it is a special test for those called prophetically. To function in the body of Christ, we must be free from rejection and its companion, the fear of man. **"The fear of man brings a snare" (see Proverbs 29:25)** and those called prophetically must be free of it. God's Word to Jeremiah is true for those who minister prophetically today.

> **Thou therefore gird up thy loins, and arise, and speak unto them all that I command thee: be not dismayed at their faces, lest I confound thee before them (Jeremiah 1:17 KJV).**

In this verse, the word **"confound"** means *to cause to fall down flat because of fear and confusion.* One snare the fear of man brings is confusion. If prophetic people fear those they minister to, confusion will overwhelm them, crippling their ability to minister. Because of the unique nature of the prophetic ministry and the disposition of those God often calls into it, rejection and the fear of man tend to be unusually prevalent in their lives.

THE REVOLVING DOOR OF REJECTION

Rejection is widespread among those called prophetically for many reasons. For some, rejection was their launching pad to becoming prophetic. After years of rejection from people, they find God as a Friend who will never leave or forsake them. By spending increasing amounts of time with Him, they begin to know things prophetically as God reveals His secrets to them. When they prophesy what God has revealed, they often experience more rejection, which drives them closer to God. This cycle is then repeated, bringing more revelation and more rejection.

Others are called by God to an unusual lifestyle of preparation, including long periods of prayer, fasting, and separation from other people. This can easily lead to misunderstanding and rejection from friends and family. The Lord will place other requirements and restraints on some to prepare them for ministry, bringing them more rejection as well. Still others experience rejection as they begin to unknowingly speak prophetically to their friends and family.

Rejection is a specific test for those called prophetically. The Lord's plan is to deliver us from specific character flaws including anger, fear, and the need for human approval. These character flaws will keep us from fulfilling our ministry. The enemy's scheme is to reinforce these character flaws in the fabric of our being. Both God and Satan want to accomplish their objectives through rejection. How we respond to rejection determines whose purposes are accomplished.

Understanding and overcoming rejection is especially necessary at this time. Many prophetic people who have been hidden while in preparation are now being accepted by the church. However, being accepted in ministry does not heal the rejection that many harbor. It often does the opposite because they know they are only being accepted for what they can do and not for who they are.

If you are a prophetic person, you must become honest quickly and learn to deal with rejection. If you are a pastor or congregational leader, you must understand these factors to help those under your care who are prophetic. If the emerging prophetic ministry is to fulfill its place, we must all be open and honest in dealing with rejection and its byproducts.

A DRAMATIC EXAMPLE

There is a profound example of the need to pass the test of rejection found in I Kings 13:1-6. This passage is one of the strangest in the Bible and not readily understood. However, it contains important insights for all those called to prophetic ministry.

> **Now behold, there came a man of God from Judah to Bethel by the word of the LORD, while Jeroboam was standing by the altar to burn incense.**
>
> **And he cried against the altar by the word of the LORD, and said, "O altar, altar, thus says the LORD, 'Behold, a son shall be born to the house of David, Josiah by name; and on you he shall sacrifice the priests of the high places who burn incense on you, and human bones shall be burned on you.'"**
>
> **Then he gave a sign the same day, saying, "This is the sign which the LORD has spoken, 'Behold, the altar shall be split apart and the ashes which are on it shall be poured out.'"**
>
> **Now it came about when the king heard the saying of the man of God, which he cried against the altar in Bethel, that Jeroboam**

stretched out his hand from the altar, saying, "Seize him." But his hand which he stretched out against him dried up, so that he could not draw it back to himself.

The altar also was split apart and the ashes were poured out from the altar, according to the sign which the man of God had given by the word of the LORD.

And the king answered and said to the man of God, "Please entreat the LORD your God, and pray for me, that my hand may be restored to me." So the man of God entreated the LORD, and the king's hand was restored to him, and it became as it was before.

REJECTION PART I—ANGER

Many prophetic people today are angry, and some are even bitter at current leaders due to rejection from previous leaders. We can see that the man of God from I Kings 13 had overcome this character flaw of anger. In verse 6 when the king's hand withered, he implored the young man to seek God for his healing. This request was from a king who was leading God's people into idolatry, and had just commanded his soldiers to arrest and probably kill the young man!

If this young man had been a bitter, wounded, unhealed prophet, he would have said, "How *dare* you seek God, you backslidden king! Seek your pagan gods, and see if they can heal you! God will *not* heal you, seeing you have left Him and have lead the people of God astray. From this day, until you are gathered to your fathers, you will not lift up nor stretch forth your hand against any man again."

But this was not his response. Instead, he sought the Lord, and the Lord restored the king's hand. The man of God had overcome rejection in that he did not take the king's reaction against him personally. Not only was he not angered, but he sought the Lord on behalf of the king. How many of us are willing to seek God on behalf of those who seek our harm? Blessing those who curse us and praying for those who despitefully use and persecute us is a requirement if we want to be like the Lord (see Matthew 5:44-48).

Many today interpret their own anger, born of past rejection, as God's wrath against others. Even some of Jesus' disciples struggled with this. When the Samaritans would not allow them to pass through their country, James and John wanted to call down fire from heaven and destroy them. Anger has caused many to miss their ultimate calling, including Moses as we have already discussed.

REJECTION PART II—THE NEED FOR HUMAN APPROVAL

Then the king said to the man of God, "Come home with me and refresh yourself, and I will give you a reward."

But the man of God said to the king, "If you were to give me half your house I would not go with you, nor would I eat bread or drink water in this place.

"For so it was commanded me by the word of the LORD, saying, 'You shall eat no bread, nor drink water, nor return by the way which you came.'"

So he went another way, and did not return by the way which he came to Bethel.

Now an old prophet was living in Bethel; and his sons came and told him all the deeds which the man of God had done that day in Bethel; the words which he had spoken to the king, these also they related to their father.

So he went after the man of God and found him sitting under an oak; and he said to him, "Are you the man of God who came from Judah?" And he said, "I am."

Then he said to him, "Come home with me and eat bread."

And he said, "I cannot return with you, nor go with you, nor will I eat bread or drink water with you in this place.

"For a command came to me by the word of the LORD, 'You shall eat no bread, nor drink water there; do not return by going the way which you came.'"

And he said to him, "I also am a prophet like you, and an angel spoke to me by the word of the LORD, saying, 'Bring him back with you to your house, that he may eat bread and drink water.'" But he lied to him.

So he went back with him, and ate bread in his house and drank water.

Now it came about, as they were sitting down at the table, that the word of the LORD came to the prophet who had brought him back;

and he cried to the man of God who came from Judah, saying, "Thus says the LORD, 'Because you have disobeyed the command of the LORD, and have not observed the commandment which the LORD your God commanded you,

but have returned and eaten bread and drunk water in the place of which He said to you, "Eat no bread and drink no water"; your body shall not come to the grave of your fathers.'"

And it came about after he had eaten bread and after he had drunk, that he saddled the donkey for him, for the prophet whom he had brought back.

Now when he had gone, a lion met him on the way and killed him, and his body was thrown on the road, with the donkey standing beside it; the lion also was standing beside the body (I Kings 13:7-11, 14-24).

Continuing through the story, we find our man of God passed another test by refusing a financial reward offered by the king. He also rejected the political opportunity to wine and dine at the king's table. But later, he disobeyed God's command and turned aside to eat with an old prophet. What caused him to rebuff the king's lucrative offer, but allowed an old prophet with nothing to offer, to deceive him?

At no point in this saga was the young man of God identified as a prophet. Yet the old prophet referred to him as such in verse 18. This young man, perhaps having endured years of misunderstanding, was now being accepted for who and what he was called to be. Whether it was subtle flattery or genuine encouragement from the old prophet does not matter. The need for acceptance as a prophet caused him to disobey God at the cost of his life.

We cannot look for our honor or acceptance from people. This is one devastating result of the fear of man. Until we are freed from the desire to please men, we are not free to serve God without entanglements. Paul, the Apostle, understood that this was the key to being Christ's slave: **"If I were still trying to please men, I would not be the bond-servant of Christ" (see Galatians 1:10).**

Jesus had also spoken this truth when He told the Pharisees, **"How can ye believe, which receive honour one of another, and seek not the honour that cometh from God only? (John 5:44 KJV)** It is impossible to have true faith and to obey God without reservation if we are looking to men for honor. This young man, full of potential for God, died a premature death because of his need for approval.

Rejection Part III—Insecurity

Another thing that caused the man of God to disobey God was insecurity. In I Kings 13:18 the old prophet says, **"I also am a prophet like you, and an angel spoke to me by the word of the LORD."** Although he had heard clearly from God to not turn aside, when the old prophet said an angel had spoken to him, the young man was wrongly impressed and discarded what the Lord had said to him. While this may appear to be humility, it was really insecurity.

Isn't an angelic visitation more powerful than a simple word? It is a higher level of revelation, correct?

Yes, it is a higher level of revelation, but there was plenty of evidence to show that the young man had heard God clearly. Remember the rent altar, withered hand, and other signs? All of these served to confirm the rest of the Word, which was to not turn aside with *anyone*. We are responsible to obey God when He speaks clearly to us, regardless of what others think or say.

We do need to listen to wise and godly counsel, but that is not the issue here. The man of God heard clearly, the rest of the word was confirmed and already fulfilled, and then he directly disobeyed the Lord through insecurity and the need for acceptance. No one in Israel had a more dramatic entrance into prophetic ministry than this man. His end could have been much greater than his beginning, but his life ended prematurely because he was not completely healed of previous rejection.

This is possibly the most dramatic introduction of any prophetic person in Israel's history. As one of the most unusual passages in Scripture, it holds key understandings for those called to prophetic ministry.

THE SOURCE OF LIFE

Rejection comes so that we might learn what is truly important. When rejection comes to us and affects us, it only reveals that we are trusting in others or their opinions. Instead of being deceived into trying to gain acceptance from those people, we need to recognize that we have fallen from looking to God alone for our acceptance.

Feeling rejected is a wonderful indicator that we have allowed our allegiance to be shifted from God to men. We can quickly repent and even be thankful for the rejection that we experience. If we understand its purpose, we can keep our attention focused on God alone for our approval.

There is only One whose approval is unchanging. It is a trap and a snare to receive honor, acceptance, or approval from any person. If our encouragement comes from people, then they are the ones we are worshiping. If it comes from God alone, then He is the focus of our worship and service.

When rejection comes, we should rejoice in God and be thankful that He is delivering us from the fear of man. Do not fall to seeking more approval from other men. Let any feelings of rejection serve to reveal that your heart already has gone astray in looking for acceptance outside of God. Turn back to Him, and you will find an approval so deep that you can obey His will, regardless of the price it may cost.

Chapter Thirteen

A WORD TO PROPHETIC PEOPLE

When I first began to move prophetically, I did not even realize that prophecy existed. I was raised in a very traditional, evangelical church environment which was void of any understanding of spiritual gifts. I eventually rebelled against the church and the Lord, choosing my own path instead.

As a sophomore in college, God began to draw me to Himself. This was not an overnight dealing because my heart was covered in pride, rebellion, and independence. Over a two-year period, God challenged the foundations of my life and confronted my sinful ways and attitudes. In the process, I became involved in a devotional way with God. I also joined an intercessory prayer ministry at my conservative, evangelical church.

While serving in this intercessory prayer ministry, I began to "know" things that had happened, were happening, or would happen to certain people for whom I prayed. I would then use this information I received from God to pray more specifically for these situations, and I began to see results which I thought were astounding.

During this time, our pastor began teaching some truths from the Bible that I had never heard and my heart was captured. This culminated in an encounter where I was baptized in the Holy Spirit, healed of a physical condition, and delivered of a demonic oppression in a five minute span. Obviously, this launched me even further in my devotional and working relationship with the Lord.

Although I had been receiving divine revelation from God while praying for others, I never really considered myself prophetic, probably because I did not know what "prophetic" meant. However, within days of this encounter with God, I began to know things about people and situations that I could not know naturally. Although this had happened before while I was praying, I was now receiving revelation outside of the prayer times, in normal, everyday life.

I remember distinctly the first instance when I spoke the secrets of a friend's heart to him. We were both stunned, because we knew that God had told me what was transpiring with him. It so shocked me that I began researching the Bible to discover what was happening. I discovered that I had received a word of knowledge, and from that point, God began teaching me about the prophetic.

In the process, God spoke to me about a calling in the prophetic ministry, although I possessed no real understanding of what that meant practically. I then began to pray for and study the prophetic gifts and ministry, but I found no real guidance except from the Bible, the Holy Spirit, and friends who were as spiritually immature as I.

I grew spiritually, made some mistakes, became frustrated, quit ministering out of embarrassment at times, and went through a good amount of rejection. I was asked to leave a church or two, was blamed for things I did not do, and was as immature as you would expect anyone with my background, prophetic gift, and stubbornness to be. I also married during this time.

In addition to my wife, God began placing others in my life who could help me. Men such as Rick Joyner, Robin McMillan, and Bob Jones were able to disciple me through their example and friendship. They loved me, gave me opportunities to minister, and confronted me when I needed it. I eventually began to prophetically function in a way that was beneficial to the church, and God opened doors for me to minister beyond our local congregation.

But in the midst of all my failures and successes, one thing never left me. I never forgot that I became prophetic simply by pursuing God and serving others through intercessory prayer. Indeed, I later found in Scripture that the foundation of most prophetic ministry is friendship with God and intercession for others.

The Place of the Word

Additionally, after being baptized in the Holy Spirit, I found the Bible to be a brand new book. I had been reading it for years, but things began making sense to me in a way that I had not previously understood. I also developed such a love for the Bible that I could not stand to be away from it for very long. Though devotion and intercession were my entrance into the prophetic, devouring the written Word served to provide the framework and structure for my understanding.

Scripture is our **"more sure word of prophecy" (see II Peter 1:19 KJV),** and if we want to be prophetic, we, like other prophetic people before us, must eat the scroll (see Ezekiel 3:14; Revelation 10:8-11). As I gave myself to studying and applying the Scriptures to my life, God began "speaking" to me, not only for individuals, but also for congregations, cities, and nations. Hiding the Word in my heart caused me to understand God's prophetic purposes in a much deeper way.

GOD'S ECONOMY

Anyone who paves streets with gold is extravagant. However, God is also economical. He seems to delight in accomplishing several things in our lives at once. In my case, as I was growing in my knowledge of the Lord, I was also growing in a sensitivity that prepared me to move prophetically. Then as I became more prophetic, I also became more deeply connected to the Lord in a devotional way by being amazed at the revelation He shared with me.

Our seeking to become prophetic should lead us to a greater devotion to the Lord Himself. If it does not, then we need to make serious adjustments in our approach. What profit is there in becoming the most prophetically gifted person on the planet if we have left our first love? This chapter is not a call to *not* pursue the gifts, but rather a reminder to pursue them *with* the Lord, not instead of Him.

Lastly, remember that we are all still learning. Do not ever fall to acting like an expert or believing that you are one. The greatest prophets of our day are still only seeing in glimpses and fragments. We must find more humility and a deeper hunger for God. We need greater revelation, greater interpretation, greater character, and greater love. We must find the heart which Paul had in order to go further in God.

That I may know him, and the power of his resurrection, and the fellowship of his

sufferings, being made conformable unto his death (Philippians 3:10 KJV).

This is the heart the Lord is looking for in us: first, that our foremost desire is to know *Him*; second, that we long to know the power of His resurrection (the empowerment He has for us); third, that we are willing to share in His sufferings and be rejected as He was; finally, that we are willing to lay down our lives for our friends, just as He laid down His life.

God is not only looking for people who can speak His words—He is looking for those who love His Son with all they have. If our lives are focused on these four issues (knowing Him, walking in His power, participating in His suffering, and laying our lives down for others), we will not only prophesy with our mouths, but also with our lives.

Chapter Fourteen

A WORD TO PASTORS AND LEADERS

I have written this book from a unique perspective. I am both a pastor and a prophetic minister. I am one of you *and* one of them. As a pastor, I understand the responsibility and difficulties associated with overseeing a large number of people with vastly different backgrounds, ideas, and callings. However, as a prophetic man, I understand from experience the misunderstandings and accompanying rejection surrounding my gift and calling.

I know there is tension between some pastors and prophetic people. Much of it is deserved. But I know your heart. You, like me, want a mature, healed prophetic ministry functioning in the congregations we serve. But to have mature prophetic people we must accept and help the immature prophetic people who are among us. Indeed, God has already sent the mature prophetic people we need; they have just come in "seedling form."

As such, we need to allow them to "be planted and staked out," giving them sufficient support to hold them in place. They need to be staked out to allow them to be rooted so that they can grow, but we cannot do this with malice, only with love. Also, we cannot prune them prematurely, or we may kill them. Many may need some time to mature before they can endure the pruning they will need.

Listed below are several encouragements to you as you open your congregation to begin moving in prophecy.

1) Value and honor the prophetic.

Teach on the prophetic. We cannot expect anything but weeds to grow unless we plant good seed. Value and honor the prophetic ministry in your teaching from the pulpit. If you will sow good seed and water and fertilize it, God will give you a good harvest.

2) Give the prophetic a place in your congregation.

Prophecy is especially helpful because it builds the church. I have seen so many people helped by the release of the prophetic that it is impossible to estimate the eternal fruit. When people see that God will use them to minister to others, many of their own struggles fall away.

3) Do not be so openminded that when you bend over your brain falls out.

Judge prophecy. Resist the temptation to be afraid of missing God. Many pastors and church leaders are hesitant to judge prophecy for fear of missing something God is saying. God is a Father and is patient with us as we grow in our understanding. If you are not sure about something, ask God and He will give you wisdom.

4) Pastor the prophetic, but do not try to make them pastors.

You cannot make an apple into an orange. People with a prophetic calling on their lives are often different and sometimes very different. They may be frustrating at times for a number of reasons. They need some of what you have, but they will never be pastors.

5) Take authority when you need to.

Don't be a wimp. Do not let the rebellious and immature run the church. This does not honor God, nor will it release the prophetic. Use wisdom and discernment in those you promote to positions of leadership.

If you teach on and release the prophetic in your congregation, you have the right to correct and discipline when needed. By building relationships of trust, the prophetic people in your congregation will be open to your correction.

There is no way to estimate the fruit that our congregation and others worldwide have experienced through a release of the prophetic. Remarkably, we have seen few real problems with those whom we have trained through our local congregation and fellowship of ministries. While our teams have ministered to over thirty thousand people prophetically through conferences, retreats, and at our church fellowship, we have encountered less than two dozen problems. While other mistakes may have occurred, they have been insignificant enough that people have not bothered to mention them.

The structure of our training has been much like the outline of this book. We teach scriptural concepts about the prophetic while removing the myths that served as obstacles. We teach how God speaks, how to interpret, and how to administrate prophecy as well. Then, we release those who have been trained to minister prophetically within the parameters listed in I Corinthians 14:3. We also use those who are more experienced and mature to lead and oversee prophetic ministry teams.

As the team members mature, we also address the different issues listed in the later chapters of this book. We teach on the spirit of prophecy, love, patience, and other fruits of the Spirit. We also deal with the rejection that some harbor and suffer from. Through it all, we try to love and receive those whom God has sent to us. We also do not hesitate to confront them personally when necessary.

But when we do confront them, we do not reject them. Possibly more than anything, the loving confrontations without rejection have brought healing to many.

Many who were immature only a few years ago are now being used by God to train and teach others. Some are now pastoring congregations and being used powerfully by God in other aspects of ministry. Give the prophetic a chance, but do not leave it to chance. Release it with purpose and planning, and you will be amazed by what happens.

WHAT ABOUT "THUS SAITH THE LORD"?

Having been raised in the conservative, evangelical church culture, I never heard anyone say, "Thus saith the Lord" until after I graduated from college. For the first two years of my walk in the Spirit, I believed I had missed out on my opportunity to be truly prophetic because I could not figure out how to give prophetic words this way. I once tried to give a prophetic word in the first person and felt so ridiculous, I simply quit speaking in the middle of the prophecy.

Before I establish a biblical position on saying, "Thus saith the Lord" when we prophesy, I need to make this disclaimer: It would be tragic to dismiss a true prophetic word because of the package in which it arrives. Just as Israel was one nation with twelve tribes, the church is also one nation made up of many different tribes. As such, there are cultural differences within the church which we should never mock, but instead respect and enjoy.

Although we ask our prophetic people not to use this designation, I would never openly correct someone who gave a true prophetic word in our congregation if they used, "Thus saith the Lord" in their prophecy. My point is not to split theological hairs, but is rather to provide helpful instruction for prophesying in a way that people can receive.

The following are my reasons for not saying, "Thus saith the Lord," when I prophesy. Each of these is based on scriptural precedents.

1) The Old Testament prophets who declared, "Thus saith the Lord," were speaking for the Lord Jehovah in the midst of many false prophets speaking in the name of their gods. Scripture lists false prophets of many different pagan deities. Baal, Ashteroth, Peor, Dagon, Molech, and other false gods all had their own prophets. Each would declare for whom they were speaking: "Thus saith the lord Baal," or "Thus saith the lord Peor." The prophets of God would also declare for whom they spoke by saying, "Thus saith the Lord Jehovah."

   When we speak prophetically within the church, it is understood that we are giving a word that we believe is from God. As such, we have no need to attach this phrase to our prophecy.

   If a believer is standing in a spiritual battle against astrologers or soothsayers who all prophesy in the name of demons they may be channeling, that is a different story. Whenever there is more than one "god" being spoken for, we must make clear the one for whom we are speaking. At that point, we may need to declare, "This is what Jesus has to say."

2) The second reason I do not say, "Thus saith the Lord" is taken from an examination of Jesus' life. The Son of God did not use this phrase when He prophesied. He only used the phrase, "Verily, verily" or in modern language, "I honestly tell you the truth."

My thinking is this: If Jesus, who was God, did not say, "Thus saith the Lord," I am not saying it either. He is our example for all ministry.

3) Last, the only time anyone in the New Testament used the phrase "Thus saith the Lord," they were inaccurate in their prophecy. Agabus used this phrase, **"Thus saith the Holy Ghost" (see Acts 21:10-11 KJV)**, and apparently misinterpreted some of the details of his revelation (see chapter four of this book for more details). If the only person to say, "Thus saith the Lord" when prophesying in the New Testament got some details wrong, then I believe that is a message for us.

Because we know in part and prophesy in part, I do not believe we should say, "Thus saith the Lord" when we prophesy. We encourage the people we train to say things like, "I believe the Lord wants you to know," or, "I feel like God has shown me something for you." This allows the person receiving the word to judge the word without putting pressure on them to accept that it is the word of the Lord, just because we say so.

Strategic Water

MST MISSION II: ZAO LIFE PROJECT

Every 8 seconds a child dies from water related diseases. We are helping to solve the problem with natural and spiritual water for Africa.

*W*e invite you to partner with us to help save a continent both physically and spiritually. Africa will know the power and love of our God. MST is our **MorningStar Strategic Team**, our fellowship of partners who give monthly and help support the missions of MorningStar, like ZAO. There is no minimum contribution amount.

SUPPORT STRATEGIC MISSIONS.

Join the Team.

For more information or to join MST:
- Call us at 1-800-542-0278
- Visit us online at
  MST.MORNINGSTARMINISTRIES.ORG
- Write to us at 375 Star Light Drive,
  Fort Mill, SC 29715

MST
MorningStar Strategic Team
PARTNERS SUPPORTING MISSIONS

RESTORED AND ALIVE AGAIN

H.I.M. CONFERENCE CENTER

In the mid 1980s, Heritage USA and PTL Ministries was one of the most celebrated locations in the world. After the PTL era, Heritage sat desolate until 2004 when MorningStar purchased the Grand Hotel, Main Street, and Conference Center. Now ministries, churches, and Christians from around the world are coming back. **Consider hosting your conference or retreat at historic Heritage.**

H.I.M. RETREAT CENTER

The newly restored property now hosts five international ministries, all within walking distance of H.I.M. Guest rooms are available for those wishing to attend any weekly service, conference, or to those who are just seeking a personal retreat. **Reserve your room today.**

For reservations and information:

- Call us at 1-800-542-0278
- Visit us online at www.HeritageInternational.org
- Write to us at 375 Star Light Drive, Fort Mill, SC 29715

Nearly 200 Rooms Have Been Sponsored

Nearly 200 H.I.M. retreat rooms have been sponsored through The Nehemiah Project. Would you like to join with us?

VIEW AVAILABLE ROOMS THROUGH A PANORAMIC VIEW:
WWW.HERITAGEINTERNATIONAL.ORG

JOIN THIS IMPORTANT PROJECT FOR THESE TIMES
- Call us at 1-800-542-0278
- Visit us online at www.HeritageInternational.org
- Write us at 375 Star Light Drive, Fort Mill, SC 29715